Black Classics

The Book of Life

sojourner truth

Published by *Black Classics*
An imprint of The X Press
6 Hoxton Square, London N1 6NU
Tel: 0171 729 1199
Fax: 0171 729 1771
Email: vibes@xpress.co.uk
Web site: www. xpress.co.uk

Printed by LEGO of Italy

Distributed in US by INBOOK, 1436 West Randolph Street, Chicago, Illinois 60607, USA Orders 1-800 626 4330 Fax orders 1-800 334 3892

Distributed in UK by Turnaround Distribution, Unit 3, Olympia Trading Estate, Coburg Road, London N22 6TZ
Tel: 0181 829 3000
Fax: 0181 881 5088

ISBN 1-874509-95-6

A PREFACE
(which was intended for a postscript)

SOJOURNER TRUTH once remarked, in reply to an allusion to the late Horace Greeley "You call him a self-made man; well, I am a self-made woman."

The world is ever ready to sound the praises of the so-called self-made men (i.e. those men who in the full possession of freedom, lacking nothing but wealth, achieve distinction and success). It is now asked to accord a modicum of honor to a woman who labored forty long and weary years a slave; to whom the paths of literature and science were forever closed; one who bore the double burdens of poverty and the ban of caste, yet who, despite all these disabilities, has acquired fame and gained hosts of friends among the noblest and best of the dominant race. The reasons for presenting the history of this remarkable woman to the public are twofold.

First, that the world, and more especially the young, may be benefited by the wisdom of one who escaped unscathed from the consuming fires of slavery, as did Shadrach, Meshach, and Abednego from the flames of the fiery furnace.

In the autumn of 1876, a report of her decease was widely circulated. But Sojourner grandly outrode the storm. Her mind is as clear and vigorous as in middle age. Her finely molded form is yet unbent, and its grand height and graceful, wary movements, remind the observer of her lofty cousins the palm trees, which keep guard over the sacred streams where her forefathers idled away their childhood days.

Doubtless, her blood is fed by those tropical fires which had slumberingly crept through many generations, but now awaken in her veins; akin to those rivers which mysteriously disappear in the bosom of the desert, and unexpectedly burst forth in springs of pure and living water. This heritage, and the law of the survival of the fittest, may explain the secret of her longevity.

The pages of this book are reprinted from stereotype plates made in 1850. Since then, momentous changes have taken place. Slavery has been swallowed up in a Red Sea of blood, and the slave has emerged from the conflict of races transformed from a chattel to a man. Holding the ballot, the black man enters the halls of legislation, and his rights are recognized where 'God is not dead', and in looking back to the Egypt of their captivity, Sojourner sees that her people have been guided through the dark wilderness of oppression by the pillar of cloud and fire.

Her race now stands on the edge of freedom,

looking into the promised land, where the culture which has so long been denied them can, by their own efforts, be obtained.

Sojourner has stood before this nation many years, advocating the cause of human rights, and yet she presses on, feeling that her century of toil does not exonerate her from the service of her Divine Master, while his *"Come labor in my vineyard,"* is responded to by so few.

Her sun of life is about to dip below the horizon; but flashes of wit and wisdom still emanate from her soul, like the rays of the natural sun as it bursts forth from a somber cloud, baptizing earth and sky with the radiance of its expiring glory.

Bishop Haven says, "There is no more deserving lady in the land than Sojourner Truth. As one of the famous women of these famous times, covering in her own experience the emancipation era, from the declaration of New York in 1817, to Abraham Lincoln's proclamation, she deserves especial honor. The nation could rightfully grant her a pension for her services in the war, no less than for her labors since the war, for the amelioration of those yet half enslaved."

The second and most important reason for offering this book to the public is, that by its sale she may be kept from want in these her last days. Should it prove a success, the desired end will be accomplished.

The following letter appeared in the *Anti Slavery Standard* after the first issue of the *The Book of Life of Sojourner Truth:*

Battle Creek, Mich.,Apr. 14, 1863

Dear Friend

Permit me, through the columns of The Standard, on behalf of Sojourner Truth, whom your readers so well remember, to acknowledge the receipt of the several donations from her many generous friends, all of which have been gratefully received by her. Printed words can never convey such deep and heartfelt gratitude as she feels. The donors needed but to have seen the expression of her dark, careworn face and heard her words of genuine thankfulness, to have realized that indeed it is 'more blessed to give than to receive'.

As we opened the letters, one by one, and read the words of sweet remembrance and kindness, she was quite overcome with joy, and more than once gave utterance to her feelings through her tears; praising the Lord who had so soon answered her prayer, which was, in language from the depth of her soul, as she sat weary and alone in her quiet little home: "I'm too old to work, too sick to hold meetings and speak to the people and sell my books; Lord, you sent the ravens to feed 'Lijah in the wilderness; send the good angels to feed me while I live on my footstool."

No sooner had the appeal gone forth, than the answers came from the East and West, accompanied with material aid to supply her physical needs. Then again she exclaimed in words of deepest gratitude: "Lord, I knew thy laws was sure, but I didn't think they would work so quick."

The words of friendship and sympathy that filled every letter were a source of great joy and consolation to her, and when the comforting message from Gerrit Smith came, saying, "Sojourner, the God whom you so faithfully serve will abundantly bless you, he will suffer you to lack nothing either in body or soul," she threw up her hands, and in her deep-toned voice, said, "The Lord bless the man! His heart is as big as the nation, and if he hadn't sent a penny, his words would feed my soul, and that is what we all want."

She mentioned Samuel Hill, of Northampton, Mass., where she lived fifteen years, saying that his noble, generous heart had done a great deal for her. Ofttimes the ecstasy of her soul would gush forth in all its original vigor and freshness at the thought of her many friends and their quick responses. She once said to me, "I tell you, chile, the Lord manages everything; you see when you wrote that letter, you didn't think you was doing much, but I tell you, dear lamb, that when a thing is done in the right spirit, God takes it up and spreads it all over the country."

She wishes the friends to know that the "little curly-headed, jolly grandson," whom Mrs. Stowe so graphically describes, is now grown to a tall, able-bodied lad, and has just enlisted in the 54th Massachusetts Regiment; gone forth with her prayers and blessings, she says, "to redeem the white people from the curse that God has sent upon them." The glorious news of old Massachusetts leading for the right of the colored man to fight, has just reached here, and she seems at times to be filled with all the fire and enthusiasm of her former years. She says if she were only ten years younger, she would be "on hand as the Joan of Arc to lead the army of the Lord; now is the hour for the colored man to save this nation; for their sin is so great that they don't know God, nor God don't know them."

I never heard her speak with greater force and power than she did the other day when some friends called to see her. She says this is all the way she has now to preach.

She often speaks of T. W. Higginson and Frances D. Gage, believing that "they are appointed of God to fill the position they have taken."

As I closed the interview, Sojourner called down many blessings on all who have helped her to live *and "do good in the world."*

I will give the names of the donors, so far as I know them. If any have sent whose names do not appear, perhaps they will write.

Yours truly,

Phebe H. M. Stickney

At the time the foregoing letter was received in 1863, Sojourner thought herself too old and infirm to either labor or lecture. But as the war of the Rebellion (which was then stirring the pulses of the nation so deeply) progressed, she experienced a new baptism, so to speak, of physical and mental vigor, which enabled her to take an active part in many of its stirring scenes. She received her commission from Abraham Lincoln, and labored in the hospitals and among the freedmen four years.

Since the war, her life has been one of activity. Now, in 1878, she oversees her own household matters, and often gives three public lectures in a week. Within the past year, she has held meetings in thirty-six towns in Michigan. Her health is good; her eyesight, for many years defective, has returned. Her gray locks are being succeeded by a luxuriant growth of black hair, without the use of any other renovator than that which kind Nature furnishes. She hopes that natural teeth will supersede the necessity of using false ones. May her ardent wish be realized! Her mental capacities are becoming intensified. A Chicago lady wrote to her, asking for a thought to inspire and cheer her on her life journey. Sojourner responded as follows:

> *God is from everlasting to everlasting.*
> *There was no beginning till sin came.*
> *All that had a beginning will have an end.*
> *Truth burns up error*
> *God is the great house that will hold all his children.*
> *We dwell in him as the fishes in the sea*

Of the fashionable so-called religious world she says, "It is empty as the barren fig-tree, possessing nothing but leaves."

This is Sojourner Truth at a century old. Would you like to meet her?

Frances Gage, 1878

SOJOURNER TRUTH'S ADDRESS TO THE AMERICAN EQUAL RIGHTS ASSOCIATION

My friends, I am rejoiced that you are glad, but I don't know how you will feel when I get through.

I come from another field — the country of the slave. They have got their liberty — so much good luck to have slavery partly destroyed; not entirely. I want it root and branch destroyed. Then we will all be free indeed. I feel that if I have to answer for the deeds done in my body just as much as a man, I have a right to have just as much as a man. There is a great stir about colored men getting their rights, but not a word about the colored women; and if colored men get their rights, and not colored women theirs, you see the colored men will be masters over the women, and it will be just as bad as it was before. So I am for keeping the thing going while things are stirring; because if we wait 'til it is still, it will take a great while to get it going again. White women are a great deal smarter, and know more than colored women, while colored women do not know scarcely anything. They go out washing, which is about as high as a colored woman gets, and their men go about idle, strutting up and down; and when the women come home, they ask for their money and take it all, and then scold because there is no food. I want you to consider on that, children. I call you children; you are somebody's children, and I am old enough to be mother of all that is here. I want women to have their rights. In the courts women have no right, no voice; nobody speaks for them. I wish woman to have her voice there among the pettifoggers. If it is not a fit place for women, it is unfit for men to be there, too.

I am above eighty years old; it is about time for me to be going. I have been forty years a slave and forty years free, and would be here forty years more to have equal rights for all. I suppose I am kept here because something remains for me to do; I suppose I am yet to help to break the chain. I have done a great deal of work; as much as a man, but did not get so much pay. I used to work in the field and bind grain, keeping up with the cradler, but men doing no more, got twice as much pay; so with the German women. They work in the field and do as much work, but do not get the pay. We do as much, we eat as much, we want as much.

I suppose I am about the only colored woman that goes about to speak for the rights of the colored women. I want to keep the thing stirring, now that the ice is cracked. What we want is a little money. You men know that you get as much again as women when you write, or for what you do. When we get our rights we shall not have to come to you for money, for then we shall have money enough in our own pockets; and maybe you will ask us for money. But help us now until we get it. It is a good consolation to know that when we have got this battle once fought we shall not be coming to you any more. You have been having our rights so long, that you think, like a slaveholder, that you own us. I know that it is hard for one who has held the rein for so long to give up; it cuts like a knife. It will feel all the better when it closes up again. I have been in Washington about three years, seeing about these colored people. Now colored men have the right to vote. There ought to be equal rights now more than ever, since colored people have got their freedom.

THE BOOK OF LIFE

"The things I want to tell you, I can not tell the men. Where there is so much wailing, there must be something not right. I think that 'twixt the niggers and the women all talkin' 'bout rights, the white man is in a fix.

But what's all this talkin' 'bout? That man over there says that women need to be helped into carriages, and lifted over ditches, and to have the best place everywhere. Nobody ever helps me into carriages, or over mud puddles, or gives me any best place, and ar'n't I a woman? Look at me! Look at my arm. I have plowed, and planted, and gathered into barns, and no man could better me, and ar'n't I a woman? I could work as much and eat as much as a man (when I could get it), and bear the lash as well, and ar'n't I a woman?

I have borne thirteen children and seen 'em sold off into slavery, and when I cried out with a mother's grief, none but Jesus heard. And ar'n't I a woman? Then they talks 'bout this thing in the head — 'intellect'. What's that got to do with women's rights or niggers' rights? S'pose a man's mind holds a quart, an a woman's don't hold but a pint; if my cup won't hold but a pint and yours holds a quart, wouldn't you

1

be mean not to let me have my little half-measure full? Then
that little man back there says women can't have as much
rights as man, cause Christ wasn't a woman.

Where did your Christ come from? From God and a
woman. Man had nothing to do with him. If the first woman
God ever made was strong enough to turn the world upside
down, all by herself, women together ought to be able to turn
it back and get it right side up again. And now they is asking
to do it, the men better let 'em."

The subject of this biography, Sojourner Truth, as she
now calls herself but whose name, originally, was
Isabella was born, as near as she can now calculate,
between the years 1797 and 1800. She was the daughter
of James and Betsey, slaves of one Colonel Ardinburgh,
Hurley, Ulster County, New York.

Colonel Ardinburgh belonged to that class of people
called Low Dutch.

Of her first master, she can give no account, as she
must have been a mere infant when he died; and she,
with her parents and some ten or twelve other fellow
human chattels, became the legal property of his son,
Charles Ardinburgh. She distinctly remembers hearing
her father and mother say, that their lot was a fortunate
one, as Master Charles was the best of the family,
comparatively speaking, a kind master to his slaves.

James and Betsey having, by their faithfulness, docility and respectful behaviour won his particular regard, received from him particular favors, among which was a lot of land, lying back on the slope of a mountain, where, by improving the pleasant evenings and Sundays, they managed to raise a little tobacco, corn, or flax; which they exchanged for articles of food or clothing for themselves and children. She has no remembrance that Saturday afternoon was ever added to their own time, as it is by *some* masters in the Southern States.

Among Isabella's earliest recollections was the removal of her master, Charles Ardinburgh, into his new house, which he had built for a hotel, soon after the death of his father. A cellar, under this hotel, was assigned to his slaves, as their sleeping apartment, all the slaves he possessed, of both sexes, sleeping (as is quite common in a state of slavery) in the same room. She carries in her mind, to this day, a vivid picture of this dismal chamber; its only lights consisting of a few panes of glass, through which she thinks the sun never shone, but with thrice reflected rays; and the space between the loose boards on the floor and the uneven earth below was often filled with mud and water, the uncomfortable splashings of which were as annoying as its noxious vapors must have been chilling and fatal to health.

She shudders, even now, as she goes back in memory, and revisits this cellar and sees its inmates, of both sexes and all ages, sleeping on those damp boards, like the horse, with a little straw and a blanket; and she wonders not at the rheumatisms, fever sores and palsies that distorted the limbs and racked the bodies of those fellow-slaves in after-life.

Still, she does not attribute this cruelty, for cruelty it certainly is, to be so unmindful of the health and comfort of any being, leaving entirely out of sight his more important part, his everlasting interests, so much to any innate or constitutional cruelty of the master, as to that gigantic inconsistency, that inherited habit among slaveholders, of expecting a willing and intelligent obedience from the slave, because he is a MAN.

At the same time everything belonging to the soul-harrowing system does its best to crush the last vestige of a man within him; and when it is crushed, and often before, he is denied the comforts of life, on the plea that he knows neither the want nor the use of them, and because he is considered to be little more or little *less* than a beast.

Isabella's father was very tall and straight when young, which gave him the name of 'Bomefree' (low Dutch for tree) at least, this is Sojourner's pronunciation of it, and by this name he usually went. The most familiar appellation of her mother was 'Mau-mau Bett'. She was the mother of some ten or twelve children (though Sojourner is far from knowing the exact number of her brothers and sisters) she being the youngest, save one, and all older than herself having been sold before her remembrance. She was privileged to behold six of them while she remained a slave.

Of the two that immediately preceded her in age (a boy of five years and a girl of three, who were sold when she was an infant) she heard much; and she wishes that all who would fain believe that slave parents have real affection for their offspring could have listened as *she* did, while Bomefree and Mau-mau Bett, their dark cellar lighted by a blazing pine-knot, would sit for hours, recalling and recounting every endearing, as well as harrowing circumstance that taxed memory could supply, from the histories of those dear departed ones, of whom they had been robbed, and for whom their hearts still bled.

Among the rest, they would relate how the little boy, on the last morning he was with them, arose with the birds, kindled a fire, calling for his Mau-mau to come, for all was now ready for her, little dreaming of the dreadful separation which was so near at hand, but of which his parents had an uncertain, but all the more cruel foreboding.

There was snow on the ground, at the time of which we are speaking; and a large old-fashioned sleigh was seen to drive up to the door of the late Col. Ardinburgh This event was noticed with childish pleasure by the unsuspicious boy; but when he was taken and put into the sleigh, and saw his little sister actually shut and locked into the sleigh box, his eyes were at once opened to their intentions; and, like a frightened deer he sprang from the sleigh and, running into the house, concealed himself under a bed. But this availed him little. He was re-conveyed to the sleigh, and separated for ever from those whom God had constituted his natural guardians and protectors, and who should have found him, in return, a stay and a staff to them in their declining years.

But I make no comments on facts like these knowing that the heart of every slave parent will make its own comments, involuntarily and correctly, as soon as each heart shall make the ease its own.

Those who are not parents will draw their conclusions from the promptings of humanity and philanthropy. These, enlightened by reason and revelation, are also unerring.

Isabella and Peter, her youngest brother, remained with their parents, the legal property of Charles Ardinburgh till his decease, which took place when Isabella was near nine years old.

After this event, she was often surprised to find her mother in tears. When, in her simplicity, Isabella inquired, "Mau-mau, what makes you cry?" she would answer, "Oh, my child, I am thinking of your brothers and sisters that have been sold away from me." And she would proceed to detail many circumstances respecting them. But Isabella long since concluded that it was the impending fate of her only remaining children, which her mother but too well understood even then, that called up those memories from the past, and made them crucify her heart afresh.

In the evening, when her mother's work was done, she would sit down under the sparkling vault of heaven, and calling her children to her, would talk to them of the only Being that could effectually aid or protect them. Her teachings (delivered in Low Dutch, her only language, and translated into English), ran nearly as follows:

"My children, there is a God, who hears and sees you."

"A God, mau-mau! Where does he live?" asked the children.

"He lives in the sky," she replied, "and when you are beaten, or cruelly treated, or fall into any trouble, you must ask help of him, and he will always hear and help you."

She taught them to kneel and say the Lord's prayer. She entreated them to refrain from lying and stealing, and to strive to obey their masters.

At times, a groan would escape her, and she would break out in the language of the Psalmist:

"Oh Lord, how long?"

And in reply to Isabella's question "What ails you, mau-mau?" her only answer was, "Oh, a good deal ails me. Enough ails me."

Then again, she would point them to the stars, and say, in peculiar language, "Those are the same stars, and that the same moon, that look down upon your brothers and sisters, and which they see as they look up to them, though they are ever so far away from us, and each other."

Thus, in her humble way, did she endeavor to show them their Heavenly Father, as the only being who could protect them in their perilous condition. At the same time, she would strengthen and brighten the chain of fair affection, which she trusted extended itself sufficiently to connect the widely scattered members of her precious flock. These instructions of the mother were treasured up and held sacred by Isabella, as our future narrative will show.

"*Thank God that the Stars and Stripes no longer symbolize the 'scars and stripes' upon the negroes back.*

We have been a source of wealth to this republic. Our labor supplied the country with cotton, until villages and cities dotted the enterprising North for its manufacture, and furnished employment and support for a multitude, thereby becoming a revenue to the government. Beneath a burning southern sun have we toiled, in the canebrake and the rice swamp; urged on by the merciless driver's lash, earning millions; and so highly were we valued there, that should one poor wretch venture to escape from this hell of slavery, no exertion of man or trained bloodhound was spared to seize and return him to his field of unrequited labor.

The overseer's horn awoke us at the dawning of day from our half-finished slumbers to pick the disgusting worm from the tobacco plant, which was an added source of wealth. Our tears and blood have been sacrificed on the altar of this nation's avarice. Our unpaid labor has been a stepping stone to its financial success. Some of its dividends must surely be ours.

Our nation will yet be obliged to pay; sigh for sigh, groan for groan, and dollar for dollar, to this wronged and outraged race. What an awful debt when we consider that interest will surely be added. Does this nation realize that the debt is still unpaid, the note not taken up yet ?

The United States owns countless acres of unoccupied land. Why not give a tract of land to those colored people who would rather become independent through their own exertions than longer clog the wheels of government? Also, the money expended upon officials to convict and punish colored children, would be ample to provide for them homes with all the necessary requirements of civilization. With God's blessing, they might yet become an honor to the country which has so cruelly wronged them."

At length, the never to be forgotten day of the terrible auction arrived, when the slaves, horses, and other cattle of Charles Ardinburgh, deceased, were to be put under the hammer, and again change masters. Not only Isabella and Peter, but their mother, was now destined to the auction block, and would have been struck off with the rest to the highest bidder, but for the following circumstance: A question arose among the heirs, "Who shall be burdened with Bomefree, when we have sent away his faithful Mau-mau Bett?" He was becoming

weak and firm; his limbs were painfully rheumatic and
distorted- more from exposure and hardship than from
old age, though he was several years older than Mau-
mau Bett: he was no longer considered of value, but
must soon be a burden and care to someone. After some
contention on the point at issue, none being willing to
be burdened with him, it was finally agreed, as most
expedient for the heirs that the price of Mau-mau Bett
should be sacrificed, and she receive her freedom, on
condition that she take care of and support her faithful
James. Faithful, not only to her as a husband, but
proverbially faithful as a slave to those who would not
willingly sacrifice a dollar for *his* comfort, now that he
had commenced his descent into the dark vale of
decrepitude and suffering. This important decision was
received as joyful news indeed to our ardent couple,
who were the objects of it, and who were trying to
prepare their hearts for a severe struggle and one
altogether new to them, as they had never before been
separated; for, though ignorant, helpless, crushed in
spirit, and weighed down with hardship and cruel
bereavement, they were still human, and their human
hearts beat within them with as true an affection as ever
caused a human heart to beat. And their anticipated
separation now, in the decline of life, after the last child
had been torn from them, must have been truly

appalling.

Another privilege granted them that of remaining occupants of the same dark, humid cellar I have before described: otherwise, they were to support themselves as they best could. And as her mother was still able to do considerable work, and her father a little, they got on for some time very comfortably. The strangers who rented the house were humane people, and very kind to them; they were not rich and owned no slaves.

How long this state of things continued, we are unable to say, as Isabella had not then sufficiently cultivated her organ of time to calculate years, or even weeks or hours. But she thinks her mother must have lived several years after the death of Master Charles. She remembers going to visit her parents some three or four times before the death of her mother, and a good deal of time seemed to her to intervene between each visit.

At length her mother's health began to decline. A fever-sore made its ravages on one of her limbs, and the palsy began to shake her frame, still, she and James tottered about, picking up a little here and there, which, added to the mites contributed by their kind neighbor sufficed to sustain life, and drive famine from the door.

One morning, in early autumn, (from the reason above mentioned, we cannot tell what year,) Mau-mau Bett told James she would make him a loaf of rye-bread, and get Mrs. Simmons, their kind neighbor, to bake it for them, as she would bake that forenoon. James told her he had engaged to rake after the cart for his neighbors that morning; but before he commenced, he would pole off some apples from a tree near, which they were allowed to gather; and if she could get some of them baked with the bread, it would give it a nice relish for their dinner. He beat off the apples, and soon after, saw Mau-mau Bett come out and gather them up.

At the blowing of the horn for dinner, he groped his way into his cellar, anticipating his humble, but warm and nourishing meal; when, lo! instead of being cheered by the sight and odor of fresh-baked bread and the savory apples, his cellar seemed more cheerless than usual, and at first neither sight nor sound met eye or ear. But, on groping his way through the room, his staff, which he used as a pioneer to go before, and warn him of danger, seemed to be impeded in its progress, and a low, gurgling, choking sound proceeded from the object before him, giving him the first intimation of the truth as it was, that Mau-mau Bett, his bosom companion, the only remaining member of his large family, had fallen in a fit of the palsy, and lay helpless and senseless on the earth!

Who among us, located in pleasant homes, surrounded with every comfort, and so many kind and sympathizing friends, can picture to ourselves the dark and desolate state of poor old James, penniless, weak, lame, and nearly blind, as he was at the moment he found his companion was removed from him, and he was left alone in the world, with no one to aid, comfort, or console him, for she never revived again, and lived only a few hours after being discovered senseless by her poor bereaved James.

Isabella and Peter were permitted to see the remains of their mother laid in their last narrow dwelling, and to make their bereaved father a little visit, ere they returned to their servitude. And most piteous were the lamentations of the poor old man, when, at last, *they* also were obliged to bid him "Farewell!" Juan Fernandes, on his desolate island, was not so pitiable an object as this poor lame man. Blind and crippled, he was too superannuated to think for a moment of taking care of himself, and he greatly feared no persons would interest themselves in his behalf.

"Oh," he would exclaim, "I had thought God would take me first, Mau-mau was so much smarter than I, and could get about and take care of herself. I am *so old*, and *so helpless*. What *is* to become of me? I can't do anything more. My children are all gone, and here I am left helpless and alone."

"And then, as I was taking leave of him," said his daughter, in relating it, "he raised his voice, and cried aloud like a child. *Oh, how he cried!* I HEAR it now and remember it as well as if it were but yesterday, *poor old man!* He thought *God* had done it all and my heart bled within me at the sight of his misery. He begged me to get permission to come and see him sometimes, which I readily and heartily promised him."

But when all had left him, the Ardinburghs, having some feeling left for their faithful and favorite slave, 'took turns about' in keeping him, permitting him to stay a few weeks at one house, and then a while at another, and so around. If, when he made a removal, the place where he was going was not too far off he took up his line of march, staff in hand, and asked for no assistance. If it was twelve or twenty miles, they gave him a ride. While he was living in this way, Isabella was twice permitted to visit him.

Another time she walked twelve miles, and carried her infant in her arms to see him, but when she reached the place where she hoped to find him, he had just left for a place some twenty miles distant, and she never saw him more.

The last time she did see him, she found him seated on a rock, by the road side, alone, and far from any house. He was then migrating from the house of one Ardinburgh to that of another, several miles distant. His hair was white like wool, he was almost blind, and his gait more a creep than a walk but the weather was warm and pleasant, and he did not dislike the journey. When Isabella addressed him, he recognized her voice, and was exceeding glad to see her. He was assisted to mount the wagon, was carried back to the famous cellar of which we have spoken, and there they held their last earthly conversation.

He again, as usual, bewailed his loneliness, spoke in tones of anguish of his many children, saying, "They are all taken away from me! I have now not one to give me a cup of cold water. Why should I live and not die?"

Isabella, whose heart yearned over her father, and who would have made any sacrifice to have been able to be with, and take care of him, tried to comfort, by telling him that she had heard the white folks say, that all the slaves in the State would be freed in ten years, and that then she would come and take care of him.

"I would take just as good care of you as Mau-mau would, if she was here," continued Isabella.

"Oh, my child," replied he, "I cannot *live* that long."

"Oh *do*, daddy, do live, and I will take such *good* care of you," was her rejoinder.

She now says, I thought then, in my ignorance that he *could* live, if he *would*. I just as much thought so, as I ever thought *any*thing in my life, and I *insisted* on his living: but he shook his head, and insisted he could not.

But before Bomefree's good constitution would yield either to age, exposure or a strong desire to die, the Ardinburghs again tired of him, and offered freedom to two old slaves, Caesar, brother of Mau-mau Bett, and his wife Betsey, on condition that they should take care of James. (I was about to say, 'their brother-in-law', but as slaves are nether *husbands* nor *wives* in law, the idea of their being brothers-in-law is truly ludicrous.) And although they were too old and infirm to take care of themselves (Caesar having been afflicted for a long time with fever-sores, and his wife with the jaundice), they eagerly accepted the boon of freedom, which had been the life-long desire of their souls, though at a time when emancipation was to them little more than destitution, and was freedom more to be desired by the master than the slave.

Sojourner declares of the slaves in their ignorance, that "their thoughts are no longer than my finger."

"When I was a slave I hated white people. My mother sat me down and said, 'Look up to the moon an' stars that shine upon you father an' upon you mother when you are sold far away. I asked her who had made the moon an' the stars, an' she says, 'God.' Where is God, I asked. 'Oh,' says she, 'chile, he sits in the sky, an' he hears you when you ask him when you are sold from us to make your master an' mistress good, an' he will do it.'

When we were sold, I did what my mother told me; I said, 'O God, my mother told me if I asked you to make my master an' mistress good, you'd do it.' But they didn't get good. 'Why,' says I, 'God, maybe you can't do it. Kill 'em, then.' After I made such wishes my conscience burned me. Then I would say, 'O God, don't be angry. My master made me wicked.' I often thought how people can do such abominable wicked things an' their conscience not burn them. Now, I only made wishes. I used to tell God, 'Now, God, if I was you, an' you was me, and you wanted any help I'd help you; why don't you help me?' Well, you see, I was in want, an' I felt

*that there was no help. I know what it is to be taken in the
barn an' tied up an' the blood drawn out of your bare back,
an' I tell you, it would make you think 'bout God.*

*But I got no good master until the last time I was sold, an'
then I found one an' his name was Jesus. Oh, I tell you, didn't
I find a good master when I used to feel so bad, when I used
to say, 'O God, how can I live? I'm hurting within and
without.' When God gave me that master he healed all the
wounds up. My soul rejoiced. I used to hate white people so,
an' I tell you, when the love came in me I had so much love I
didn't know what to love. Then the white people came, an' I
thought that love was too good for them. Then I said, 'Yea,
God, I'll love everybody an' the white people, too. Ever since
then, that love has continued an' kept me among white people.
Ain't it wonderful that God gives love enough to the
Ethiopians to love white people?"*

A rude cabin, in a lone wood, far from any neighbors,
was granted to our freed friends, as the only assistance
they were now to expect. Bomefree, from this time,
found his poor needs hardly supplied, as his new
providers were scarce able to administer to their *own*
wants. However, the time drew near when things were
to be decidedly worse rather than better; for they had
not been together long, before Betty died, and shortly
after, Caesar followed her to 'that place from whence no

traveller returns', leaving poor James again desolate, and more helpless than ever before; as, this time, there was no kind family in the house, and the Ardinburghs no longer invited him to their homes. Yet, lone, blind and helpless as he was, James for a time lived on. One day, an aged colored woman, named Soan, called at his shanty, and James sought her, in the most moving manner, even with tears, to tarry awhile and wash and mend him up, so that he might once more be decent and comfortable; for he was suffering dreadfully with the filth and vermin that collected upon him.

Soan was herself an emancipated slave, old and weak with no one to care for her; and she lacked t,he courage to undertake a job of such seeming magnitude, fearing she might herself get sick, and perish there without assistance; and with great reluctance, and a heart swelling with pity, as she afterwards declared, she felt obliged to leave him in his wretchedness and filth. And shortly after her visit, this faithful slave, this deserted wreck of humanity, was found on his miserable pallet, frozen and stiff in death. The kind angel had come at last, and relieved him of the many miseries that his fellow-man had heaped upon him. Yes, he had died, chilled and starved, with none to speak a kindly word, or do a kindly deed for him, in that last dread hour of need!

The news of his death reached the ears of John Ardinburgh, a grandson of the old Colonel; and he declared that Bomefree, who had ever been a kind and faithful slave, should now have a *good* funeral.

And now, gentle reader, what think you constituted a good funeral? Answer — some black paint for the coffin, and a jug of ardent spirits! What a compensation for a life of toil, of patient submission to repeated robberies of the most aggravated kind, and, also, far more than murderous neglect! Mankind often vainly attempt to atone for unkindness or cruelty to the living, by honoring the same after death; but John Ardinburgh undoubtedly meant *his* pot of paint and jug of whisky should act as an opiate on his slaves, rather than on his own seared conscience.

"Children, I talks to God and God talks to me. I goes out and talks to God in the fields and the woods. This morning I was walking out and I saw the wheat holding up its head, looking very big. I goes up and takes hold of it. I says, 'God what is the matter with this wheat?' and he says to me, 'Sojourner, there is a little weasel in it.' Now I hears talkin' about the Constitution and the rights of man. I comes up and I takes hold of this Constitution. It looks mighty big, and I feels for my rights but there ain't any there. Then I says, 'God, what is wrong with this Constitution?' He says to me, 'Sojourner, there is a little weasel in it.'

Having seen the sad end of her parents, so far as it relates to *this* earthly life, we will return with Isabella to that memorable auction which threatened to separate her father and mother. A slave auction is a terrible affair to its victims, and its incidents and consequences are graven on their hearts as with a pen of burning steel.

At this memorable time, Isabella was struck off, for

the sum of one hundred dollars, to one John Nealy, of Ulster County, New York; and she has an impression that in this sale she was connected with a lot of sheep. She was now nine years of age, and her trials in life may be dated from this period. She says, with emphasis, "*Now the war begun.*"

She could only talk Dutch, and the Nealys could only talk English. Mr. Nealy could *understand* Dutch, but Isabella and her mistress could neither of them understand the language of the other, and this, of itself was a formidable obstacle in the way of a *good* understanding between them, and for some time was a fruitful source of dissatisfaction to the mistress, and of punishment and suffering to Isabella.

"If they sent me for a frying.pan, not knowing what they meant, perhaps I carried them the pot hooks and trammels. How angry mistress would be with me!"

Then she suffered "*terribly-terribly,*" with the cold. During the winter her feet were badly frozen, for want of proper covering. They gave her a plenty to eat, and also plenty of whippings. One Sunday morning, in particular she was told to go to the barn; on going there, she found her master with a bundle of rods, prepared in the embers, and bound together with cords. When he had tied her hands together before her, he gave her the most cruel whipping she was ever tortured with. He whipped her till the flesh was deeply lacerated, and the blood streamed from her wounds and the scars remain to the present day, to testify to the fact.

She says, "When I hear 'em tell of whipping women on the bare flesh, it makes *my* flesh crawl, and my very hair rise on my head! Oh! my God! What a way is this of treating human beings?"

In these hours of her extremity, she did not forget the instructions of her mother, to go to God in all her trials, and every affliction; and she not only remembered, but obeyed: going to him, and telling Him all, and asking Him if He thought it was right, and begging him to protect and shield her from her persecutors.

She always asked with an unwavering faith that she should receive just what she pleaded for. "And now," she says "though it seems *curious*, I do not remember ever asking for any thing but what I got it. And I always received it as an answer to my prayers. When I got beaten, I never knew it long enough beforehand to pray; and I always thought if I only had *had* time to pray to God for help, I should have escaped the beating."

She had no idea God had knowledge of her thoughts, save what she told him in prayer. Consequently, she could not pray unless she had time and opportunity to be by herself where she could talk to God without being overheard.

"My name was Isabella; but when I left the house of bondage, I left everything behind. I wasn't going to keep nothin' of Egypt on me, an' so I went to the Lord an' asked him to give me a new name. And the Lord gave me Sojourner, because I was to travel up an' down the land, showing the people their sins, an' being a sign unto them. Afterward I told the Lord I wanted another name, 'cause everybody else had two names; and the Lord gave me Truth, because I was to declare the truth to the people."

When she had been at Mr. Nealy's several months, she began to beg God most earnestly to send her father to her, and as soon as she commenced to pray, she began as confidently to look for his coming, and, ere it was long, to her great joy, he came. She had no opportunity to speak of the troubles that weighed so heavily on her spirit, while he remained; but when he left, she followed him to the gate, and unburdened her heart to him inquiring if he could not do something to get her a new and better place. In this way the slaves often assist each other, by ascertaining who are kind to their slaves, comparatively; and then using their influence to get such an one to hire or buy their friends; and masters, often from policy, as well as from latent humanity, allow those they are about to sell or let, to choose their own places, if the persons they happen to select for masters are considered safe *pay*. He promised to do all he could, and they parted.

But, every day, as long as the snow lasted (for there was snow on the ground at the time), she returned to the spot where they separated, and walking in the tracks her father had made in the snow, repeated her prayer that God would help her father get her a new and better place.

A long time had not elapsed, when a fisherman by the name of Scriver appeared at Mr. Nealy's, and inquired of Isabella if she would like to go and live with him.

She eagerly answered "Yes," nothing doubting but he was sent in answer to her prayer; and she soon started off with him, walking while he rode; for he had bought her at the suggestion of her father, paying one hundred and five dollars for her. He also lived in Ulster County, but some five or six miles from Mr. Nealy's.

Scriver, besides being a fisherman, kept a tavern for

the accommodation of people of his own class, for his was a rude, uneducated family, exceedingly profane in their language, but, on the whole, an honest, kind and well-disposed people.

They owned a large farm, but left it wholly unimproved; attending mainly to their vocations of fishing and inn-keeping. Isabella declares she can ill describe the life she led with them.

It was a wild, out-of-door kind of life. She was expected to carry fish, to hoe corn, to bring roots and herbs from the wood for beers, go to the Strand for a gallon of molasses or liquor as the case might require, and browse around. It was a life that suited her well for the time being, as devoid of hardship or terror as it was of improvement; a need which had not yet become a want.

Instead of improving at this place, morally, she retrograded, as their example taught her to curse; and it was here that she took her first oath. After living with them about a year and a half, she was sold to one John J. Dumont, for the sum of seventy pounds. This was in 1810. Mr. Dumont lived in the same county as her former masters, in the town of New Paltz, and she remained with him till a short time previous to her emancipation by the State, in 1828.

Had Mrs. Dumont possessed that vein of kindness and consideration for the slaves, so perceptible in her husband's character, Isabella would have been as comfortable here, as one had *best* be, if one *must* be a slave. Mr.Dumont had been nursed in the very lap of slavery and being naturally a man of kind feelings, treated his slaves with all the consideration he did his *other* animals, and *more* perhaps. But Mrs. Dumont, who had been born and educated in a non-slaveholding family, and, like many others only to work-people, who, under the most stimulating of human motives, were willing to put forth their every energy, could not have patience with the creeping gait, the dull understanding, or see any cause for the listless manners and careless, slovenly habits of the poor downtrodden outcast, entirely forgetting that every high and efficient motive had been removed far from him; and that, had not his very intellect been crushed out of him, the slave would find little ground for aught but hopeless despondency. From this source arose a long series of trials in the life of our heroine, which we must pass over in silence; some from motives of delicacy, and others, because the relation of them might inflict undeserved pain on some now living, whom Isabella remembers only with esteem and love; therefore, the reader will not be surprised if our narrative appear somewhat tame at this point, and may rest assured that it is not for want of facts, as the most thrilling incidents of this portion of her life are from various motives suppressed.

One comparatively trifling incident she wishes related, as it made a deep impression on her mind at the time (showing, as *she* thinks, how God shields the innocent, and causes them to triumph over their enemies, and also how she stood between master and mistress). In her family, Mrs. Dumont employed two white girls, one of whom, named Kate, evinced a disposition to 'lord it' over Isabella, and, in her emphatic language, *to grind her down*. Her master often shielded her from the attacks and accusations of others, praising her for her readiness and ability to work, and these praises seemed to foster a spirit of hostility to her, in the minds of Mrs. Dumont and her white servant, the latter of whom took every opportunity to cry up her faults, lessen her in the esteem of her master and increase against her the displeasure of her mistress, which was already more than sufficient for Isabella's comfort. Her master insisted that she could do as much work as half a dozen common people, and do it well, too; whilst her mistress insisted that the first was true, only because it ever came from her hand but half performed.

A good deal of feeling arose from this difference of opinion, which was getting to rather an uncomfortable height, when, all at once, the potatoes that Isabella cooked for breakfast assumed a dingy, dirty look. Her mistress blamed her severely, asking her master to observe "a fine specimen of Bell's work," adding, "it is the way *all* her work is done."

Her master scolded also this time, and commanded her to be more careful in future.

Kate joined with zest in the censures, and was very hard upon her. Isabella thought that she had done all she well could to have them nice; and became quite distressed at these appearances, and wondered what she should do to avoid them In this dilemma, Gertrude Dumont, (Mr. D.'s eldest child, a good, kind-hearted girl of ten years, who pitied Isabella sincerely,) when she heard them all blame her so unsparingly came forward, offering her sympathy and assistance; and when about to retire to bed, on the night of Isabella's humiliation she advanced to Isabella, and told her, if she would wake her early next morning, she would get up and attend to her potatoes for her, while she (Isabella) went to milking, and they would see if they could not have them *nice*, and not have 'Poppee', her word for father, and 'Matty', her word for mother, and of 'em, scolding so terribly.

Isabella gladly availed herself of this kindness, which touched her to the heart, amid so much of an opposite spirit. When Isabella had put the potatoes over to boil Getty told her she would herself tend the fire, while Isabella milked. She had not long been seated by the fire in performance of her promise, when Kate entered, and requested Gertrude to go out of the room and do some thing for her, which she refused, still keeping her place in the corner. While there, Kate came sweeping about the fire, caught up a chip, lifted some ashes with it, and dashed them into the kettle. Now the mystery was solved, the plot discovered! Kate was working a little too at making her mistress's words good, at showing that Mrs. Dumont and herself were on the right side of the dispute, and consequently at gaining power over Isabella. Yes, she was quite too fast, inasmuch as she had overlooked the little figure of justice, which sat in the corner with scales nicely balanced, waiting to give all their dues.

But the time had come when she was to be overlooked no longer. It was Getty's turn to speak now. "Oh Poppee! oh, Poppee!" said she, "Kate has been putting ashes in among the potatoes! I saw her do it! Look at those that fell on the outside of the kettle! You can now see what made the potatoes so dingy every morning, though Bell washed them clean!" And she repeated her story to every new comer, till the fraud was made as public as the ensure of Isabella had been. Her mistress looked blank, and remained dumb. Her master muttered something which sounded very like an oath, and poor Katte was so chop-fallen, she looked like a convicted criminal who would gladly have hid herself, (now that the baseness was out,) to conceal her mortified pride and deep chagrin.

It was a fine triumph for Isabella and her master, and she became more ambitious than ever to please him; and he stimulated her ambition by his commendation, and by boasting of her to his friends, telling them that *"that wench"* (pointing to Isabella) "is better to me than a *man,* for she will do a good family's washing in the night and be ready in the morning to go into the field, where she will do as much raking and binding as my best hands." Her ambition and desire to please were so great, that she often worked several nights in succession, sleeping only short snatches, as she sat in her chair; and some nights she would not allow herself to take any sleep, save what she could get resting herself against the wall, fearing that if she sat down, she would sleep too long. These extra exertions to please; and the praises consequent upon them, brought upon her head the envy of her fellow slaves, and they taunted her with being the *"white folks' nigger."* On the other hand, she received a larger share of the confidence of her master, and many small favors that were by them unattainable. I asked her if her master, Dumont, ever whipped her? She answered, "Oh yes, he sometimes whipped me soundly, though never cruelly. And the most severe whipping he ever give me was because *I* was cruel to a cat." At this time she looked upon her master as a *God*; and believed that he knew of and could see her at all times, even as God himself And she used sometimes to confess her delinquencies, from the conviction that he already knew them, and that she should fare better if she confessed voluntarily and if any one talked to her of the injustice of her being a slave, she answered them with contempt and immediately told her master. She then firmly believed that slavery was right and honorable. Yet she *now* sees very clearly the false position they were all in, both masters and slaves; and she looks back, with utter astonishment, at the absurdity of the claims so arrogantly set up by the masters, over beings designed by God to be as free as kings; and at the perfect stupidity of the slave, in admitting for one moment the validity of these claims.

In obedience to her mother's instructions, she had educated herself to such a sense of honesty, that, when she had become a mother, she would sometimes whip her child when it cried to her for bread, rather than give it a piece secretly, lest it should learn to take what was not its own! And the writer of this knows, from personal observation, that the slaveholders of the South feel it to be a *religious duty* to teach their slaves to be honest, and never to take what is not their own! Oh consistency, art thou not a jewel? Yet Isabella glories in the fact that she was faithful and true to her master; she says "It made me true to my God," meaning, that it helped to form in her a character that loved truth, and hated a lie, and had saved her from the bitter pains and fears that are sure to follow in the wake of insincerity and hypocrisy.

As she advanced in years, an attachment sprung up between herself and a slave named Robert. But his master, an Englishman by the name of Catlin, anxious that no one's property but his own should be enhanced by the increase of his slaves, forbade Robert's visits to Isabella, and commanded him to take a wife among his fellow-servants. Notwithstanding this interdiction, Robert, following the bent of his inclinations, continued his visits to Isabella, though very stealthily, and, as he believed, without exciting the suspicion of his master; but one Saturday afternoon, hearing that Bell was ill, he took the liberty to go and see her. The first intimation *she* had of his visit was the appearance of her master,

inquiring if she had seen Bob. On her answering in the
negative, he said to her, "If you see him, tell him to take
care of himself, for the Catlins are after him." Almost at
that instant, Bob made his appearance; and the first
people he met were his old and his young masters. They
were terribly enraged at finding him there, and the
eldest began cursing, and calling upon his son to
"Knock down the damned black rascal;" at the same
time, they both fell upon him like tigers, beating him
with the heavy ends of their canes, bruising and
mangling his head and face in the most awful manner,
and causing the blood, which streamed from his
wounds, to cover him like a slaughtered beast,
constituting him a most shocking spectacle. Mr.
Dumont interposed at this point, telling the ruffians
they could no longer thus spill human blood on *his*
premises he would have "no niggers killed" there. The
Catlins then took a rope they had taken with them for
the purpose, and tied Bob's hands behind him in such a
manner, that Mr. Dumont insisted on loosening the
cord, declaring that no brute should be tied in *that*
manner, where *he* was. And as they led him away, like
the greatest of criminals, the more humane Dumont
followed them to their homes, as Robert's protector; and
when he returned he kindly went to Bell, as he called
her, telling her he did not think they would strike him

any more, as their wrath had greatly cooled before he left them. Isabella had witnessed this scene from her window, and was greatly shocked at the murderous treatment of poor Robert, whom she truly loved, and whose only crime, in the eye of his persecutors, was his affection for her. This beating, and we know not what after treatment, completely subdued the spirit of its victim, for Robert ventured no more to visit Isabella, but like an obedient and faithful, took himself a wife from the house of his master. Robert did not live many years after his last visit to Isabella, but took his departure to that country, where they neither marry nor are given in marriage and where the oppressor cannot molest.

"Well, honey, I've been to Women's Rights meetings, an' heard a good deal. They wanted me to speak. So I got up. Says I, 'Sisters, I'm not clear what you're after. If women want any rights more than they've got, why don't they just take 'em, an' not be talkin' about it?' Some of 'em came round me, an' asked why I didn't wear bloomers. An' I told 'em I had bloomers enough when I was in bondage. You see, they used to weave what they called 'nigger-cloth', an' each one of us got just such a strip, an' had to wear it width-wise. Them that was short got along pretty well, but as for me... I tell you, I had enough of bloomers in them days."

Subsequently, Isabella was married to a fellow-slave, named Thomas, who had previously had two wives, one of whom, if not both, had been torn from him and sold far away. And it is more than probable that he was not only allowed, but encouraged to take another at each successive sale. I say it is probable, because the writer of this knows from personal observation, that such is the custom among slaveholders at the present day; and that in a twenty months' residence. among them, we never knew anyone to open the lip against the practice; and when we severely censured it, the slaveholder had nothing to say; and the slave pleaded that, under existing circumstances, he could do no better.

Such an abominable state of things is silently tolerated to say the least, by slaveholders — deny it who may. And what is that religion that sanctions, even by its silence, all that is embraced in the 'peculiar institution'? If there *can* be anything more diametrically opposed to the religion of Jesus than the working of this soul-killing system, which is as truly sanctioned by the religion of America as are her ministers and churches we wish to be shown where it can be found.

We have said, Isabella was married to Thomas, she was, after the fashion of slavery, one of the slaves performing the ceremony for them; as no true minister of Christ *can* perform, as in the presence of God, what he knows to be a mere *farce*, a *mock* marriage, unrecognized by any civil law, and liable to be annulled any moment, when the interest or caprice of the master should dictate.

With what feelings must slaveholders expect us to listen to their horror of amalgamation in prospect, while they are well aware that we know how calmly and quietly they contemplate the present state of licentiousness their own wicked laws have created, not only as it regards the slave, but as it regards the more privileged portion of the population of the South?

Slaveholders appear to me to take the same notice of the vices of the slave, as one does of the vicious disposition of his horse. They are often an inconvenience; further than that, they care not to trouble themselves about the matter.

"We have heard a great deal about love at home in the family. Now, children, I was a slave, and my husband and my children was sold from me...

Now, husband and children is all gone, and what has become of the affection I had for them...?"

In process of time, Isabella found herself the mother of five children, and she rejoiced in being permitted to be the instrument of increasing the property of her oppressors!

Think, dear reader, without a blush, if you can, for one moment, of a mother thus willingly, and with pride, laying her own children, the flesh of her flesh, on the altar of slavery, a sacrifice to the bloody Moloch!

But we must remember that beings capable of such sacrifices are not mothers; they are only 'things', 'chattels', 'property'.

But since that time, the subject of this narrative has made some advances from a state of chattelism towards that of a woman and a mother; and she now looks back upon her thoughts and feelings there, in her state of ignorance and degradation, as one does on the dark imagery of a fitful dream. One moment it seems but a frightful illusion; again it appears a terrible reality. I would to God it were but a dreamy myth, and not, as it now stands, a horrid reality to some three millions of chattelized human beings.

I have already alluded to her care not to teach her children to steal, by her example; and she says, with groanings that cannot be written, "The Lord only knows how many times I let my children go hungry, rather than take secretly the bread I liked not to ask for."

All parents who annul their perceptive teachings by their daily practices would do well to profit by her example.

Another proof of her master's kindness of heart is found in the following fact. If her master came into the house and found her infant crying, (as she could not always attend to its wants and the commands of her mistress at the same time,) he would turn to his wife with a look of reproof, and ask her why she did not see the child taken care of; saying, most earnestly, "I will not hear this crying; I can't bear it, and I will not hear any child cry so. Here, Bell, take care of this child, if no more work is done for a week."

And he would linger to see if his orders were obeyed, and not countermanded.

When Isabella went to the field to work, she used to put her infant in a basket, tying a rope to each handle and suspending the basket to a branch of a tree, set another small child to swing it. It was thus secure from reptiles, and was easily administered to, and even lulled to sleep, by a child too young for other labors.

I was quite struck with the ingenuity of such a baby-tender, as I have sometimes been with the swinging hammock the native mother prepares for her sick infant, apparently so much easier than aught we have in our more civilized homes; easier for the child, because it gets the motion without the least jar; and easier for the nurse, because the hammock is strung so high as to supersede the necessity of stooping.

After emancipation had been decreed by the State, some years before the time fixed for its consummation, Isabella's master told her if she would do well, and be faithful, he would give her 'free papers', one year before she was legally free by statute.

In the year 1826, she bad a badly diseased hand, which greatly diminished her usefulness; but on the arrival of July 4, 1827, the time specified for her receiving her 'free papers', she claimed the fulfilment of her master's promise; but he refused granting it, on account (as he alleged) of the loss he had sustained by her hand. She pleaded that she had worked all the time, and done many things she was not wholly able to do, although she knew she had been less useful than formerly; but her master remained inflexible. Her very faithfulness probably operated against her now, and he found it less easy than he thought to give up the profits of his faithful Bell, who had so long done him efficient service.

But Isabella inwardly determined that she would remain quietly with him only until she had spun his wool, about one hundred pounds, and then she would leave him the rest of the time to herself.

"Ah!" she said, with emphasis that cannot be written, "the slaveholders are terrible for promising to give you this or that, or such and such a privilege, if you will do thus and so; and when the time of fulfilment comes, and one claims the promise, they, forsooth, recollect nothing of the kind; and you are, like as not, taunted with being a liar, or, at best, the slave is accused of not having performed *his* part or condition of the contract."

"Oh," said she, "I have felt as if I could not live through the operation sometimes. Just think of us, so eager for our pleasures, and just foolish enough to keep feeding and feeding ourselves up with the idea that we should get what had been thus fairly promised; and when we think it is almost in our hands, find ourselves flatly denied. Just think, how *could* we bear it?"

Why, there was Charles Brodhead promised his slave Ned, that when harvesting was over, he might go and see his wife, who lived some twenty or thirty miles off. So Ned worked early and late, and as soon as the harvest was all in, he claimed the promised boon. His master said, he had merely told him he would *see* if he could go, when the harvest was over; but now he saw that he *could not go*.

But Ned, who still claimed a positive promise, on which he had fully depended, went on cleaning his shoes. His master asked him if he intended going, and on his replying "Yes," took up a stick that lay near him, and gave him such a blow on the head as broke his skull, killing him dead on the spot.

The poor colored people all felt struck down by the blow. Ah, and well they might. Yet it was but one of a long series of bloody, and otherwise most effectual blows, struck against their liberty and their lives. Yet no official notice was taken of this brutal murder.

But to return from our digression.

The subject of this narrative was to have been free on

July 4, 1827, but she continued with her master till the wool was spun, and the heaviest of the Fall's work closed up, when she concluded to take her freedom into her own hands, and seek her fortune in some other place.

"You ask me what to do? Do you want a poor old creature who don't know how to read, to tell educated people what to do? I've given you the hint, and you ought to know what to do. But if you don't, I can tell you. Give coloured people land and teach them to read. Then they can be somebody. That's what I want. You owe it to them, because you took away all they earned and made 'em what they are. You take no interest in the colored people. I was forty years a slave in the State of New York. You are the children of those who enslaved us. That's what I want to say. I wish this hall was full to hear me. I don't want to say anything against Anna Dickinson because she is my friend, but if she came here to talk about a woman you know nothing about (Joan of Arc), and no one knows whether there really was such a woman or not, you would fill this place. You want to hear nonsense. I come to tell something which you ought to listen to. You are ready to help the heathen in foreign lands, but don't care for the heathen right about you."

The question in her mind, and one not easily solved, now was, "How can I get away?" So, as was her usual custom, she told God she was afraid to go in the night, and in the day everybody would see her. At length the thought came to her that she could leave just before the day dawned, and get out of the neighborhood where she was known before the people were much astir.

"Yes," said she, fervently, "that's a good thought! Thank you, God, for that thought!"

So, receiving it as coming direct from God, she acted upon it, and one fine morning, a little before daybreak, she might have been seen stepping stealthily away from the rear of Master Dumont's house, her infant on one arm and her wardrobe on the other; the bulk and weight of which, probably, she never found so convenient as on the present occasion, a cotton handkerchief containing both her clothes and her provisions.

As she gained the summit of a high hill, a considerable distance from her master's, the sun offended her by coming forth in all its pristine splendor. She thought it never was so light before; indeed, she thought it much too light. She stopped to look about her to ascertain if the pursuers were yet in sight. No one appeared. The question came up for settlement, "Where, and to whom, shall I go?" In all her thoughts of getting away, she had not once asked herself whither she should direct her steps. She sat down, fed her infant, and again turning her thoughts to God, her only help, she prayed him to direct her to some safe asylum. And soon it occurred to her, that there was a man living somewhere in the direction she had been pursuing, by the name of Levi Rowe, whom she had known, and who, she thought, would be likely to befriend her. She accordingly pursued her way to his house, where she found him ready to entertain and assist her, though he was then on his death-bed. He bade her partake of the hospitalities of his house, said he knew of two good places where she might get in, and requested his wife to show her where they were to be found. As soon as she came in sight of the first house, she recollected having seen it and its inhabitants before, and instantly exclaimed, "That's the place for me. I shall stop there."

She went there, and found the good people of the house, Mr. and Mrs. Van Wagener absent, but was kindly received and hospitably entertained by their excellent mother, till the return of her children. When they arrived, she made her ease known to them. They listened to her story, assuring her they never turned the needy away, and willingly gave her employment.

She had not been there long before her old master, Dumont, appeared as she had anticipated; for when she took French leave of him, she resolved not to go too far from him, and not put him to as much trouble in looking her up, for the latter he was sure to do, as Tom and Jack had done when they ran away from him a short time before. This was very considerate in her, to say the least, and a proof that 'like begets like'. He had often considered *her* feelings, though not always, and was equally considerate.

When her master saw her, he said, "Well, Bell, so you've run away from me."

"No, I did not *run* away; I walked away by daylight, and all because you had promised me a year of my time."

His reply was, "You must go back with me."

Her decisive answer was, "No, I *won't* go back with you."

He said, "Well, I shall take the *child*."

This also was as stoutly negatived.

Mr. Isaac S. Van Wagener then interposed, saying, he had never been in the practice of buying and selling slaves; he did not believe in slavery; but, rather than have Isabella taken back by force, he would buy her services for the balance of the year, for which her master charged twenty dollars, and five in addition for the child. The sum was paid, and her master Dumont departed, but not till he had heard Mr. Van Wagener tell her not to call him master, adding, "There is but *one* master; and he who is *your* master is *my* master."

Isabella inquired what she should call him?

He answered, "Call me Isaac Van Wagener, and my wife is Maria Van Wagener."

Isabella could not understand this, and thought it a mighty change, as it most truly was from a master whose word was law, to simple Isaac S. Van Wagener, who was master to no one. With these noble people who, though they could not be the masters of slaves, were undoubtedly a portion of God's nobility, she resided one year, and from them she derived the name of Van Wagener; he being her last master in the eye of the law, and a slave's surname is ever the same as his master; that is, if he is allowed to have any other name than Tom, Jack, or Guffin. Slaves have sometimes been severely punished for adding their master's name to their own. But when they have no particular title to it, it is no particular offence.

A little previous to Isabella's leaving her old master, he had sold her child, a boy of five years, to a Dr. Gedney, who took him with him as far as New York City, on his way to England. Finding the boy too small for his service, he sent him back to his brother, Solomon Gedney. This man disposed of him to his sister's husband, a wealthy planter, by the name of Fowler, who took him to his own home in Alabama.

This illegal and fraudulent transaction had been perpetrated some months before Isabella knew of it, as she was now living at Mr. Van Wagener's. The law expressly prohibited the sale of any slave out of the State, and all minors were to be free at twenty-one years of age; and Mr. Dumont had sold Peter with the express understanding, that he was soon to return to the State of New York, and be emancipated at the specified time.

When Isabella heard that her son had been sold South she immediately started on foot and alone, to find the man who had thus dared, in the face of all law, human and divine, to sell her child out of the State; and if possible, to bring him to account for the deed.

Arriving at New Paltz, she went directly to her former mistress, Dumont, complaining bitterly of the removal of her son. Her mistress heard her through, and then replied, "*Ugh!* a *fine* fuss to make about a little *nigger*. Why, haven't you as many of 'em left as you can see to and take care of? A pity 'tis, the niggers are not all in Guinea! Making such a halloo-balloo about the neigborhood; and all for a paltry nigger!"

Isabella heard her through, and after a moment's hesitation, answered intones of deep determination, "*I'll have my child again.*"

"Have *your child* again!" repeated her mistress, her tone big with contempt, and scorning the absurd idea of her getting him. "How can you get him? And what have got to support him with, if you could? Have you any money?"

"No," answered Bell, "I have no money, but God has enough, or what's better! And I'll have my child again."

These words were pronounced in the most slow, solemn and determined measure and manner. And in speaking of it, she says, "Oh, my God! I knew I'd have him again. I was sure God would help me to get him Why, I felt so *tall within,* I felt as if the power of a nation was with me!"

The impressions made by Isabella on her auditors, when moved by lofty or deep feeling, can never be transmitted to paper until we are enabled to transfer the look, the gesture, the tones of voice, in connection with the quaint, yet fit expressions used, and the spirit-stirring animation that, at such a time, pervades all she says.

After leaving her mistress, she called on Mrs. Gedney mother of him who had sold her boy; who, after listening to her lamentations her grief being mingled with indignation the sale of her son, and her declaration that she would have him again, said, "Dear me! What a disturbance to make about your child! What, is *your* child better than *my* child! My child is gone out there, and yours is gone to live with her, to have enough of everything, and to be treated like a gentleman!" And here she laughed at Isabella's absurd fears, as she would represent them to be.

"Yes," said Isabella, "*your* child has gone there, but she is *married* and my boy has gone as a *slave*, and he is too little to go so far from his mother. Oh, I must have my child."

And here the continued laugh of Mrs. G seemed to Isabella, in this time of anguish and distress, almost demonical. And well it was for Mrs. Gedney that, at that time, she could not even dream of the awful fate awaiting her own beloved daughter, at the hands of him whom she had chosen as worthy the wealth of her love and confidence, and in whose society her young heart had calculated on a happiness, purer and more elevated than was ever conferred by a kingly crown. But, alas, she was doomed to disappointment, as we shall relate by and by. At this point, Isabella earnestly begged of God that he would show to those about her that He was her helper; and she adds, in narrating, "And He *did*; or, if He did not show them, he did me."

The cause was unpopular then. The leaders of the Woman's rights movement trembled on seeing a tall, black woman, in a gray dress and white turban, surmounted by an uncouth sun-bonnet, march deliberately into the church, walk with the air of a queen up the aisle, and take her seat upon the pulpit steps. A buzz of disapprobation was heard all over the house, and such words as these fell upon listening ears:

"An abolition affair!"

"Woman's rights and niggers!"

"We told you so!"

"Go it, old darkey!"

Old Sojourner, quiet and reticent sat crouched against the wall on the corner of the pulpit stairs, her sun-bonnet shading her eyes, her elbows on her knees, and her chin resting upon her broad, hard palm.

Again and again timorous and trembling ones came forward and said with earnestness, "Don't let her speak, it will ruin us. Every newspaper in the land will have our cause mixed with abolition and niggers, and we shall be utterly denounced."

Methodist, Baptist, Episcopal, Presbyterian, and Universalist ministers came in to hear and discuss the resolutions presented. One claimed superior lights and privileges for man on the ground of superior intellect; another, because of the manhood of Christ.

"If God had desired the equality of woman, he would have given some token of his will through the birth, life, and death of the Saviour."

Another gave us a theological view of the sin of our first mother.

There were few women in those days that dared to speak at meetings, and the august teachers of the people were seeming to get the better of us, while the boys in the galleries and the sneerers among the pews were hugely enjoying the discomfiture, as they supposed, of the 'strong minded'. Some of the tender-skinned friends were on the point of losing dignity, and the atmosphere of the convention betokened a storm.

Slowly from her seat in the corner rose Sojourner Truth, who, till now, had scarcely lifted her head.

"Do not let her speak!" gasped half a dozen again.

She moved slowly and solemnly to the front, laid her old bonnet at her feet, and started speaking.

There was a hissing sound of disapprobation above and below. The tumult subsided, as every eye was fixed on this almost Amazon form, which stood nearly six feet high, head erect, and eye piercing the upper air, like one in a dream. At her first word, there was a profound hush. She spoke in deep tones, which, though not loud, reached every ear in the house, and away through the throng at the doors and windows.

She concluded her words amid roars of applause, leaving many streaming eyes and hearts beating with gratitude. She had taken her listeners up in her strong arms and carried them safely over the tide with a magical influence that subdued the mob and turned the jibes and sneers of an excited crowd into notes of respect and admiration. Hundreds rushed up to shake hands, and congratulate the glorious old mother and bid her God speed on her mission of testifying again concerning the wickedness of these men.

It is often darkest just before dawn. This homely proverb was illustrated in the case of one sufferer; for, at the period at which we have arrived in our narrative, to her the darkness seemed palpable, and the waters of affliction covered her soul; yet light was about to break in upon her.

Soon after the scenes related in our last chapter, which had harrowed up her very soul to agony, she met a man, (we would like to tell you *who*, dear reader, but it would be doing him no kindness, even at the present day, to do so), who evidently sympathized with her and counselled her to go to the Quakers, telling her they were all feeling very indignant at the fraudulent sale of her son and assuring her that they would readily assist her, and direct her what to do. He pointed out to her two houses, where lived some of those people, who formerly, more than any other sect, perhaps, lived out the principles of the gospel of Christ. She wended her way to their dwellings, was listened to, unknown as she personally was to them, with patience, and soon gained their sympathies and active co-operation.

They gave her lodgings for the night; and it is very amusing to hear her tell of the "nice, high, clean, white, *beautiful* bed" assigned her to sleep in, which contrasted so strangely with her former pallets, that she sat down and contemplated it, perfectly absorbed in wonder that such a bed should have been appropriated to one like herself. For some time she thought that she would lie down beneath it, on her usual bedstead, the floor. "I did, indeed," says she, laughing heartily at her former self. However, she finally concluded to make use of the bed, for fear that not to do so might injure the feelings of her good hostess. In the morning, the Quaker saw that she was taken and set down near Kingston, with directions to go to the Court House, and enter complaint to the Grand Jury.

By a little inquiry, she found which was the building

she sought, went into the door, and taking the first man she saw of imposing appearance for the *grand* jury, she commenced her complaint. But he very civilly informed her there was no Grand Jury there; she must go up stairs. When she had with some difficulty ascended the flight through the crowd that filled them, she again turned to the *'grandest'* looking man she could select, telling him she had come to enter a complaint to the Grand Jury. For his own amusement he inquired what her complaint was; but, when he saw it was a serious matter, he said to her, "This is no place to enter a complaint, go in there," he said, pointing in a particular direction.

She went in, where she found the Grand Jurors indeed sitting, and again commenced to relate her injuries. After holding some conversation among themselves, one of them rose, and bidding her follow him, led the way to a side office, where he heard her story, and asked her "if she could *swear* that the child she spoke of was her son."

"Yes," she answered, "I swear it"s my son."

"Stop, stop!" said the lawyer, "you must swear by this book."

He handed her a book, which she thinks must have been the Bible. She took it, and putting it to her lips, began again to swear it was her child. The clerks, unable to preserve their gravity any longer, burst into an uproarious laugh; and one of them inquired of lawyer Chip of what use it could be to make her swear. "It will answer the law," replied the officer. He then made her comprehend just what be wished her to do, and she took a lawful oath, as far as the outward ceremony could make it one. All can judge how far she understood its spirit and meaning.

He now gave her a writ, directing her to take it to the constable of New Paltz, and have him serve it on Soloman Gedney. She obeyed, walking, or rather *trotting*, in her haste, some eight or nine miles.

But while the constable, through mistake, served the writ on a brother of the real culprit, Solomon Gedney slipped into a boat, and was nearly across the North River, on whose banks they were standing, before the Dutch constable was aware of his mistake. Soloman Gedney, meanwhile, consulted a lawyer, who advised him to go to Alabama and bring back the boy, otherwise I might cost him fourteen years' imprisonment, and a thousand dollars in cash. By this time, it is hoped he began to feel that selling slaves unlawfully was not so good a business as he had wished to find it. He secreted himself till due preparations could be made, and soon set sail for Alabama Steamboats and railroads had not then annihilated distance to the extent they now have, and although he left in the fall of the year, spring came ere he returned, bringing the boy with him but holding on to him as his property. It had ever been Isabella's prayer, not only that her son might be returned, but that he should be delivered from bondage, and into her own hands, lest he should be punished out of mere spite to her, who was so greatly annoying and irritating to her oppressors; and if her suit was gained, her very triumph would add vastly to their irritation.

She again sought advice of Esquire Chip, whose counsel was, that the aforesaid constable serve the before mentioned writ upon the right person. This being done, soon brought Solomon Gedney up to Kingston, where he gave bonds for his appearance at court, in the sum of $600.

Esquire Chip next informed his client, that her case must now lie over till the next session of the court, some months in the future. "The law must take its course," said he.

"What! wait another court! wait *months*," said the persevering mother. "Why, long before that time, he can go clear off, and take my child with him, no one knows where. I *cannot* wait; I *must* have him *now*, whilst he is to be had."

"Well," said the lawyer, very coolly, "if he puts the boy out of the way, he must pay the $600, one half of which will be yours;" supposing, perhaps, that $300 would pay for a heap of children, in the eye of a slave who never, in all her life, called a dollar her own. But in this instance, he was mistaken in his reckoning. She assured him, that she had not been seeking money, neither would money satisfy her; it was her son, and her son alone she wanted, and her son she must have. Neither could she wait court, not she. The lawyer used his every argument to convince her, that she ought to be very thankful for what they had done for her; that it was a great deal, and it was but reasonable that she should now wait patiently the time of the court.

Yet she never felt, for a moment like being influenced by these suggestions. She felt confident she was to receive a full and literal answer to her prayer, the burden of which had been:

"O Lord, give my son into my hands, and that speedily! Let not the spoilers have it any longer."

Notwithstanding, she very distinctly saw that those who had thus far helped her on so kindly were *wearied* of her, and she feared God was wearied also. She had a short time previous learned that Jesus was a Saviour, and an intercessor; and she thought that if Jesus could but be induced to plead for her in the present trial, God would listen to *him*, though he were wearied of *her* importunities. To him, of course, she applied. As she was walking about scarcely knowing whither she went, asking within herself, "Who will show me any good, and lend a helping hand in this matter," she was accosted by a perfect stranger, and one whose name she has never learned, in the following terms: "Halloo, there; how you get along with your boys do they give him up to you?" She told him all, adding that now everybody was tired, and she had none to help her. He said, here! I'll tell you what you'd better do. Do you see that stone house yonder?" pointing in a particular direction. "Well, Lawyer Demain lives there, and do you go to him, and lay your case before him; I think he'll help you. *Stick to him*. Don't give him peace till he does. I feel sure if you press him, he'll do it for you." She needed no further urging, but trotted off at her peculiar gait in the direction of his house, as fast as possible, and she was not encumbered with stockings, shoes, or any other heavy article of dress. When she had told him her story, in her impassioned manner, he looked at her a few moments, as if to ascertain if he were contemplating a new variety of the genus homo, and then told her, if she would give him five dollars, he would get her son for her, in twenty-four hours. "Why," she replied, "*I* have no *money*, and never had a dollar in my life."

Said he "If you will go to those Quakers in Poppletown, who carried you to court, they will help you to five dollars in cash, I have no doubt; and you shall have your son in twenty-four hours, from the time you bring me that sum." She performed the journey to Poppletown, a distance of some ten miles, very expeditiously; collected considerable more than the sum specified by the barrister; then, shutting the money tightly in her hand, she trotted back, and paid the lawyer a larger fee than he had demanded. When inquired of by people what she had done with the overplus, she answered, "Oh. I got it for lawyer Demain, and I gave it to him." They assured her she was a *fool* to do so; that she should have kept all over five dollars, and purchased herself shoes with it. "Oh, I do not want money or clothes now, I only want my son; and if five dollars will get him, more will *surely* get him." And if the lawyer had returned it to her, she avers she would have accepted it. She was perfectly willing he should have every coin she could raise, if he would but restore her lost son to her.Moreover, the five dollars he required were for the remuneration of him who should go after her son and his master, and not for his own services.

The lawyer renewed his promise, that she should have her son In twenty-four hours But Isabella, having no idea of this space of time, went several times in a day, to ascertain if her son had come. Once, when the servant opened the door and saw her, she said, in a tone expressive of much surprise, "Why, this woman's come again!" She then wondered if she went too often. When the lawyer appeared, he told her the twenty-four hours would not expire till the next morning; if she would call then, she would see her son. The next morning saw Isabella at the lawyer's door, while he was yet in his bed. He now assured her it was morning till noon; and that before noon her son would be there, for he had sent the famous Matty Styles after him, who would not fail to have the boy and his master on hand in due season, either dead or alive; of that he was sure. Telling her she need not come again; he would himself inform her of their arrival.

After dinner, he appeared at Mr. Rutzer's, (a place the lawyer had procured for her, while she awaited the arrival of her boy,) assuring her, her son had come; but that he stoutly denied having any mother, or any relatives in that place; and said, she must go over and identify him.

She went to the office, but at sight of her the boy cried aloud, and regarded her as some terrible being, who was about to take him away from a kind and loving friend. He knelt, even, and begged them, with tears, not to take him away from his dear master, who had brought him from the dreadful South, and been so kind to him.

When he was questioned relative to the bad scar on his forehead, he said, Fowler's horse hoofed him. And of the one on his cheek, "That was done by running against the carriage." In answering these questions he looked imploringly at his master, as much as to say, "If they are falsehoods, you bade me say them; may they be satisfactory to you, at least."

The justice, noting his appearance, bade him forget his master and attend only to him. But the boy persisted in denying his mother, and clinging to his master, saying his mother did not live in such a place as that. However, they allowed the mother to identify her son; and Esquire Demain pleaded that he claimed the boy for her, on the ground that he had been sold out of the State, contrary to the laws in such cases made and provided, spoke of the penalties annexed to said crime, and of the sum of money the delinquent was to pay, in case any one chose to prosecute him for the offence he had committed. Isabella, who was sitting in a corner, scarcely daring to breathe, thought within herself "If I can but get the boy, the $200 may remain for whoever else chooses to prosecute, *I* have done enough to make myself enemies already", and she trembled at the thought of the formidable enemies she had. Probably arrayed against herself, helpless and despised as she was. When the pleading was at an end, Isabella understood the Judge to declare, as the sentence of the Courts that the boy be delivered into the hands of the mother, having no other master, no other controller, no other conductor, but his mother.

This sentence was obeyed; he was delivered into her hands, the boy meanwhile begging, most piteously, *not* to be taken from his dear master, saying she was not his mother, and that his mother did not live in such a place as that. And it was some time before lawyer Demain, the clerks, and Isabella, could collectively succeed in calming the child's fears, and in convincing him that Isabella was not some terrible monster, as he had for the last months, probably, been trained to believe; and who in taking him away from his master, was taking him from all good, and consigning him to all evil.

When at last kind words and *bon bons* had quieted his fears, and he could listen to their explanations, he said to Isabella, "Well, you *do* look like my mother *used* to;" and she was soon able to make him comprehend some of the obligations he was under, and the relation he stood in, both to herself and his master. She commenced as soon as practicable to examine the boy, and found, to her utter astonishment, that from the crown of his head to the sole of his foot, the callosities and indurations on his entire body were most frightful to behold. His back she described as being like her fingers, as she laid them side by side.

"Heavens! what is all *this?*" said Isabella.

He answered;, "It is where Fowler whipped, kicked, and beat me"

She exclaimed, "Oh, Lord Jesus, look, see my poor child! Oh Lord, 'render unto them double' for all this. Oh my God! Pete, how *did* you bear it?"

"Oh, this is nothing, mammy, if you should see Phillis, I guess you'd *scare!* She had a little baby, and Fowler cut her till the milk as well as blood ran down *her* body. You would *scare* to see Phillis, mammy."

When Isabella inquired "What did Miss Eliza say, Pete, when you were treated so badly?" he replied, "Oh, mammy, she said she wished I was with Bell. Sometimes I crawled under the stoop, mammy, the blood running all about me, and my back would stick to the boards; and sometimes Miss Eliza would come and grease my sores, when all were abed and asleep."

As soon as possible she procured a place for Peter, as tender of locks, at a place called Wahkendall, near Greenkills After he was thus disposed of, she visited her sister Sophia, who resided at Newburg, and spent the winter in several different families where she was acquainted. She remained some time in the family of a Mr. Latin, who was a visiting relative of Solomon Gedney; and the latter, when he found Isabella with his cousin, used all his influence to persuade him she was a great mischief-maker and a very troublesome person, that she had put him to some hundreds of dollars expense, by fabricating lies about him, and especially his sister and her family, concerning her boy, when the latter was living so like a gentleman with them; and, for his part, he would not advise his friends to harbor or encourage her. However, his cousins, the Latins, could not see with the eyes of *his* feelings, and consequently his words fell powerless on them, and they retained her in their service as long as they had aught for her to do.

She then went to visit her former master, Dumont She scarcely arrived there, when Mr. Fred. Waring entered, and seeing Isabella, pleasantly accosted her, and asked her what she was driving at nowadays. On her answering "nothing particular," he requested her to go over to his place, and assist his folks, as some of them were sick, and they needed an extra hand. She very gladly assented. When Mr W. retired, her master wanted to know why she wished to help people, that called her the 'worst of devils', as Mr. Waring had done in the court-house, for he was the uncle of Solomon Gedney, and attended the trial we have described, and declared that she was a *fool* to; *he* wouldn't do it.

"Oh," she told him, she would not mind that, but was very glad to have people forget their anger towards her.

She went over, but too happy to feel that their resentment was passed, and commenced her work with a light heart and a strong will. She had not worked long in this frame of mind, before a younger daughter of Mr. Waring rushed into the room, exclaiming, with uplifted hands, "Heavens and earth, Isabella! Fowlers murdered Cousin Eliza!"

"Ho," said Isabella, *"that's* nothing, he liked to have killed *my* child; nothing saved him but God." Meaning, that she was not at all surprised at it, for a man whose heart was sufficiently hardened to treat a mere child as hers had been treated, was, in her opinion more fiend than human, and prepared for the commission of any crime that his passions might prompt him to. The child further informed her, that a letter had arrived by mail bringing the news.

Immediately after this announcement, Solomon Gedney and his mother came in, going direct to Mrs. Waring's room, where she soon heard tones as of someone reading. She thought something said to her inwardly, 'Go up stairs and hear'.

At first she hesitated, but it seemed to press her the

more, 'Go up and hear!'

She went up and, unusual as it is for slaves to leave their work and enter unbidden their mistress's room, for the sole purpose of seeing or hearing what may be seen or heard there, on this occasion Isabella says, she walked in through the door, shut it, placed her back against it and listened. She saw them and heard them read"

"He knocked her down with his fist, jumped on her with his knees, broke her collar bone, and tore out her wind-pipe! He then attempted his escape, but was pursued and arrested, and put it in an iron bank for safe-keeping!" And the friends were requested to go down and take away the poor innocent children who had thus been made in one short day more than orphans.

If this narrative should ever meet the eye of those innocent sufferers for another's guilt, let them not be too deeply affected by the relation; but, placing their confidence in Him who sees the end from the beginning, and controls the results, rest secure in the faith, that, although they may physically suffer for the sins of others, if they remain but true to themselves, their highest and more enduring interests can never suffer from such a cause. This relation should be suppressed for their sakes, were it not even now so often denied, that slavery is fast undermining all true regard for human life. We know this one instance is not a demonstration to the contrary, but, adding this to the lists of tragedies that weekly come up to us through the Southern mails, may. we not admit them as proof irrefragable? The newspapers confirm this account of the terrible affair.

When Isabella had heard the letter, all being too much absorbed in their own feelings to take note of her, she returned to her work, her heart swelling with conflicting emotions She was awed at the dreadful deed; she mourned.the fate of the loved Eliza, who had in such an undeserved and barbarous manner been put away from her labors and watchings as a tender mother; and, last though not least, in the development of her character and spirit, her heart bled for the afflicted relatives; even those of them who laughed at her calamity, and mocked when her fear came. Her thoughts dwelt long and intently on the subject, and the wonderful chain of events that had conspired to bring her that day to that house, to listen to that piece of intelligence, to that house, where she never was before or afterwards in her life, and invited there by people who had so lately been hotly incensed against her. It all seemed very remarkable to her, and she viewed it as flowing from a special providence of God. She thought

she saw clearly, that their unnatural bereavement was a
blow dealt in retributive justice: but she found it not in
her heart to exult or rejoice over them. She felt as if God
had more than answered her petition, when she
ejaculated, in her anguish of mind, "Oh, Lord, render
unto them double!" She said, "I dared not find fault
with God, exactly; but the language of my heart was,
'Oh, my God ! that's too much, I did not mean quite so
much, Lord. 'It was a terrible blow to the friends of the
deceased; and her selfish mother (who, said Isabella,
made such a 'to-do about *her* boy not from affection,
'but to have her own will and way') went deranged, and
walking to and fro in her delirium called aloud for her
poor murdered daughter: "Eliza! Eliza!"

The derangement of Mrs. G. was a matter of hearsay,
as Isabella saw her not after the trial; but she has no
reason to doubt the truth of what she heard. Isabella
could never learn the subsequent fate of Fowler, but
heard in the spring of '49 that his children had been seen
in Kingston, one of whom was spoken of as a fine,
interesting girl, albeit a halo of sadness fell like a veil
about her.

The Lord has made me a sign unto this nation, an' I go round a-testifyin' an' showin' on 'em their sins against my people. I can't preach from the Bible, can't read a letter. When I preaches, I have just one text to preach from, an' I always preaches from: 'WHEN I FOUND JESUS.'

Well, now, I'll just have to go back an' tell you all about it. You see we was all brought over from Africa, father an' mother an' I, an' a lot more of us; an' we was sold up an' down, an' hither an' yon; an' I can 'member, when I was a little thing, how my ole mammy would sit outside in the evenin' an' look up at the stars an' groan. She'd groan an' groan, an' says I to her, 'Mammy, what makes you groan so?'

An' she'd say, 'Matter enough, chile, I'm groanin' to think of my poor children. They don't know where I be, an' I don't know where they be; they look up at the stars, an' I look up at the stars, but I can't tell where they be. Now,' she said, 'chile, when you're grown up, you may be sold away from your mother an' all your old friends, an' have great troubles come on you; an' when you have these troubles come on you, you just go to God, an' he'll help you.'

An says I to her, 'Who is God, anyhow, mammy?'

An' says she, 'Why, chile, you just look up there. It's him that made all them.'

Well, I didn't mind much 'bout God in them days. I grew up pretty lively an' strong, an' could row a boat, or ride a horse, or work round, an' do 'most anything.

Eventually I got sold away to a real hard massa an' missis. Oh, I tell you, they was hard! 'Peared like I couldn't please 'em no how. An' then I thought of what my old mammy told me about God, an' I thought I'd got into trouble, sure enough, an' I wanted to find God, an' I heard someone tell a story about a man that met God on a threshin'-floor, an' I thought, well an' good, I'll have a threshin'-floor, too. So I went down in the lot, and I threshed down a place real hard, an' I used to go down there every day, an' pray an' cry with all my might, a-prayin' to the Lord to make my master an' missis better, but it didn't seem to do no good; and so says I, one day, "O God, I been a-askin' you, an' askin' you, an askin' you, for all this long time, to make my massa an' missis better, an' you don't do it, an' what can be the reason? Why, maybe you can't. Well, I shouldn't wonder if you couldn't. Well, now, I tell you, I'll make a bargain with you. If you'll help me to git away from my massa an' missis, I'll agree to be good; but if you don't help me, I really don't think I can be. Now,' says I, 'I want to git away; but the trouble's just here; if I try to git away in the night, I can't see; an' if I try to git away in the daytime, they'll see me an' be after me.'

Then the Lord said to me, 'Git up two or three hours afore daylight, an' start work.'

An' says I, 'Thank you, Lord. That's a good thought.'

"So up I got about three o'clock in the mornin', an' I started an' traveled pretty fast, when the sun rose, I was clear away from our place an' our folks, an' out of sight. An' then I begun to think I didn't know nothin' where to go. So I kneeled down, and says I, 'Well Lord, you've started me out, an' now please show me where to go.'

Then the Lord made a house appear to me, and he said to me that I was to walk on till I saw that house, an' then go in an' ask the people to take me.

An' I traveled all day, an' didn't come to the house until late at night; but when I saw it, sure enough, I went in, an' I told the folks that the Lord sent me; an' they was Quakers, an' real kind they was to me. They just took me in an' did for me as kind as if I'd been one of 'em; an' after they'd given me supper, they took me into a room where there was a great, tall, white bed; an' they told me to sleep there. Well, honey, I was kind of scared when they left me alone with that great white bed; 'cause I never had been in a bed in my life. It never came into my mind they could mean me to sleep in it. An' so I just camped down under it, on the floor, an' then I slept pretty well. In the morning, when they came in, they asked me if I hadn't been asleep; an' I said, 'Yes, I never slept better.' An' they said, 'Why, you haven't been in the bed!' An' says I, 'Laws, you didn't think of such a thing as my sleeping in that bed, did you? I never heard of such a thing in my life.'

Well, you see, honey, I stayed an' lived with 'em for two or three years, an' then the slaves in New York were all set free, an' ole massa came to our house to make a visit, an' he asked me if I didn't want to go back an' see the folks on the ole place. An' I told him I did. So he said, if I'd just git into the wagon with him, he'd carry me over. Well, just as I was goin' out to get into the wagon, I met God! An' says I, 'God, I didn't know as you was so great.' An' I turned right round an' come into the house, an' set down in my room; for it was God all around me. I could feel it burnin', burnin', burnin' all around me, an' goin' through me; an' I saw I was so wicked, it seemed as if it would burn me up. An' I said, 'O somebody, somebody, stand between God an' me, for it burns me!' Then, honey, when I said so, I felt as it were somethin' like an umbrella that came between me an' the light, an' I felt it was somebody — somebody that stood between me an' God; an' it felt cool, like a shade. An' says I, 'Who's this that stands between me an' God? Is it old Cato, he was a pious old preacher; but then I seemed to see Cato in the light, an' he was all polluted an' vile, like me; an' I said, 'Is it old Sally?' an' then I saw her, an' she seemed just so. An' then says I, 'Who is this?' An' then, honey, for a while it was like the sun shinin' in a pail of

*water, when it moves up and down; for I began to feel it was
somebody that loved me; an' I tried to know him. An' I said,
'I know you! I know you! I know you!' An' then I said, 'I
don't know you! I don't know you! I don't know you!' An'
when I said, 'I know you, I know you,' the light came; an'
when I said, 'I don't know you, I don't know you,' it went just
like the sun in a pail of water. An' finally somethin' spoke out
in me an' said, 'This is Jesus!' An' I spoke out with all my
might, an' says I, 'Glory be to God!' An' then the whole world
grew bright, an' the trees waved in glory, an' every little bit
of stone on the ground shone like glass; and I shouted an' said,
'Praise, praise, praise the the Lord!' An' I began to feel such
a love in my soul as I never felt before — love to all creatures.
An' then, all of a sudden, it stopped, an' I said, ' There's the
white folks that have abused you, an' beat you, an' abused
your people — think of them!' But then there came another
rush of love through my soul, an' I cried out loud 'Lord, Lord,
I can love even the white folks!'*

*Honey, I just walked round an' round in a dream. Jesus
loved me. I knew it, I felt it. Jesus was my Jesus. Jesus would
love me always. I didn't dare tell nobody; it was a great secret.
Everything had been got away from me that I ever had; an' I
thought that if I let white folks know about this, maybe they'd
take it away, so I said, 'I'll keep this close. I won't let anyone
know.'*

I had never been told about Jesus Christ. I hadn't heard no

preachin' or been to no meetin'. Nobody hadn't told me. I'd
kind of heard of Jesus, but thought he was like General
Lafayette, or some of them. But one night there was a
Methodist meetin' somewhere in our parts, an' I went; an'
they got up an' began for to tell their experiences, an' the first
one began to speak. He told about Jesus. 'Why,' says I to
myself, 'that man's found him, too!' An' another got up an'
spoke, an' I said, 'He's found him, too!' An' finally I said,
'Why, they all know him.' I was so happy.

We will now turn from the outward and temporal to the
inward and spiritual life of our subject. It is both
interesting and instructive to trace the exercises of a
human mind, through the trials and mysteries of life;
and especially a naturally powerful mind, left as hers
was almost entirely to its own workings, and the chance
influences it met on its way; and especially to note its
reception of that divine light, that *lighteth every man that*
cometh into the world.

We see, as knowledge dawns upon it, truth and error
strangely commingled; here, a bright spot illuminated
by truth and there, one darkened and distorted by error;
and the state of such a soul may be compared to a
landscape at early dawn, where the sun is seen superbly
gilding some objects, and causing others to send forth
their lengthened, distorted, and sometimes hideous

shadows.

Her mother, as we have already said, talked to her of God. From these conversations, her incipient mind drew the conclusion, that God was a great man, greatly superior to other men in power; and being located high in the sky, could see all that transpired on the earth. She believed he not only saw, but noted down all her actions in a great book, even as her master kept a record of whatever he wished not to forget. But she had no idea that God knew a thought of hers till she had uttered it aloud.

As we have before mentioned, she had ever been mindful of her mother's injunctions, spreading out in detail all her troubles before God, imploring and firmly trusting him to send her deliverance from them. Whilst yet a child, she listened to a story of a wounded soldier, left alone in the trail of a flying army, helpless and starving, who hardened the very ground about him with kneeling in his supplications to God for relief, until it arrived. From this narrative, she was deeply impressed with the idea, that if *she* also were to present her petitions under the open canopy of heaven, speaking very loud, she should the more readily be heard; consequently, she sought a fitting spot for this, her rural sanctuary. The place she selected, in which to offer up her daily orisones, was a small island in a small

stream, covered with large willow shrubbery, beneath
which the sheep had made their pleasant winding
paths; and sheltering themselves from the scorching
rays of a noon-tide sun, luxuriated in the cool shadows
of the graceful willows, as they listened to the tiny falls
of the silver waters. It was a lonely spot, and chosen by
her for its beauty, its retirement, and because she
thought that there, in the noise of those waters, she
could speak louder to God, without being overheard by
any who might pass that way. When she had made
choice of her sanctum, at a point of the island where the
stream met, after having been separated, she improved
it by pulling away the branches of the shrubs from the
centre, and weaving them together for a wall on the
outside, forming a circular arched alcove, made entirely
of the graceful willow. To this place she resorted daily,
and in pressing times much more frequently.

At this time, her prayers, or, more appropriately,
'talks with God', were perfectly original and unique,
and would be well worth preserving, were it possible to
give the tones and manner with the words; but no
adequate idea of them can be written while the tones
and manner remain inexpressible.

She would sometimes repeat, *Our Father in heaven* in
her Low Dutch, as taught her by her mothers, after all
was from the suggestions of her own rude mind She

related to God, in minute detail, all her troubles and sufferings, inquiring, as she proceeded, "Do you think I was right, God?" and closed by begging to be delivered from the evil, whatever it might be.

She talked to God as familiarly as if he had been a creature like herself; and a thousand times more so, than if she had been in the presence of some earthly potentate. She demanded, with little expenditure of reverence or fear, a supply of all her more pressing wants, and at times her demands approached very near to commands. She felt as if God was under obligation to her, much more than she was to him. He seemed to her benighted vision in some manner bound to do her bidding.

Her heart recoils now, with very dread, when she recalls these shocking, almost blasphemous conversations with the great Jehovah. And well for herself d d she deem it, that, unlike earthly potentates, his infinite character combined the tender father with the omniscient and omnipotent Creator of the universe.

She at first commenced promising God, that if he would help her out of all her difficulties, she would pay him by being very good; and this goodness she intended as a remuneration to God. She could think of no benefit that was to accrue to herself or her fellow-creatures from her leading a life of purity and generous self, sacrifice for the good of others; as far as any but God was concerned, she saw nothing in it but heart-trying penance, sustained by the sternest exertion; and this she soon found much more easily promised than performed.

Days wore away, new trials came, God's aid was invoked, and the same promises repeated; and every successive night found her part of the contract unfulfilled. She now began to excuse herself by telling God she could not be good in her present circumstances; but if he would give her a new place and a good master and mistress, she could and would be good, and she expressly stipulated, that she would be good *one* day to show God how good she would be *all* of the time, when he should surround her with the right influences, and she should be delivered from the temptations that then so sorely beset her. But, alas! when night came, and she became conscious that she had yielded to all her temptations, and entirely failed of keeping her word with God, having prayed and promised one hour, and fallen into the signs of anger and profanity the next, the mortifying reflection weighed on her mind, and blunted her enjoyment. Still she did not lay it deeply to heart, but continued to repeat her demands for aid, and her promises of pay, with full purpose of heart, at each particular time, that that day she would not fail to keep her plighted word.

Thus perished the inward spark, like a flame just igniting, when one waits to see whether it will burn on or die out, till the long desired change came, and she found herself in a new place, with a good mistress, and one who never instigated an otherwise kind master to be unkind to her; in short, a place where she had literally nothing to complain of, and where, for a time, she was more happy than she could well express. "Oh, everything there was so pleasant, and kind, and good, and all so comfortable; enough of everything; indeed, it was beautiful!" she exclaimed.

Here, at Mr. Van Wagener's, as the reader will readily perceive she must have been, she was so happy and satisfied, that God was entirely forgotten. Why should her thoughts turn to Him, who was only known to her as a help in trouble? She had no trouble now; her every prayer had been answered in every minute particular. She had been delivered from her persecutors and temptations, her youngest child had been given her, and the others she knew she had no means of sustaining if she had them with her, and was content to leave them behind. Their father, who was much older than Isabella, and who preferred serving his time out in slavery, to the trouble and dangers of the course she pursued, remained with and could keep an eye on them though it is comparatively little that they can do for each other while they remain in slavery; and this little the slave, like persons in every other situation of life, is not always disposed to perform. There are slaves, who, copying the selfishness of their superiors in power, in their conduct towards their fellows who may be thrown upon their mercy, by infirmity or illness, allow them to suffer for want of that kindness and care which it is fully in their power to render them.

The slaves in this country have ever been allowed to celebrate the principal, if not some of the lesser festivals observed by the Catholics and Church of England; many of them not being required to do the least service for several days, and at Christmas they have almost universally an entire week to themselves, except, perhaps, the attending to a few duties, which are absolutely required or t.he comfort of the families they belong to. If much service is desired, they are hired to do it, and paid for it as if they were free. The more sober portion of them spent these holidays in earning a little money. Most of them visit and attend parties and balls, and not a few of them spend it in the lowest dissipation. This respite from toil is granted them by all religionists, of whatever persuasion, and probably originated from the fact that many of the slaveholders were members of the Church of England.

Frederick Douglass, who has devoted his great heart
heart and noble talents entirely to the furtherance of the
cause of his down-trodden race, has said, "From what I
know of the effect of their holidays upon the slave, I
believe them to be among the most effective means, in
the hands of the slaveholder, in keeping down the spirit
of insurrection. Were the slaveholders at once to
abandon this practice, I have not the slightest doubt it
would lead to an immediate insurrection among the
slaves. These holidays serve as conductors, or safety-
valves, to carry off the rebellious spirit of enslaved
humanity. But for these, the slave would be forced up to
the wildest desperation; and woe betide the slaveholder,
the day he ventures to remove or hinder the operation
of those conductors! I warn him that, in such an event, a
spirit will go forth in their midst, more to be dreaded
than the most appalling earthquake."

When Isabella had been at Mr. Van Wagener's a few
months, she saw in prospect one of the festivals
approaching. She knows it by none but the Dutch name,
Pingster, as she calls it, but I think it must have been
Whitsuntide, in English. She says she "looked back into
Egypt and everything looked so pleasant there," as she
saw retrospectively all her former companions enjoying
their freedom for at least a little space, and in her heart
she longed to be with them. With this picture before her

mind's eye, she contrasted the quiet, peaceful life she was living with the excellent people of Wahkendall, and it seemed so dull and void of incident, that the very contrast served but to heighten her desire to return, that, at least, she might enjoy with them, once more, the coming festivities. These feelings had occupied a secret corner of her breast for some time, when one morning, she told Mrs. Van Wagener that her old master Dumont would come that day, and that she should go home with him on his return. They expressed some surprise, and asked her where she obtained her information she replied, that no one had told her, but she felt that he would come.

It seemed to have been one of those events that cast their shadows before; for, before night, Mr. Dumont made his appearance. She informed him of her intention to accompany him home. He answered, with a smile, "I shall not take you back again; you ran away from me." Thinking his manner contradicted his words, she did not feel repulsed, but made herself and child ready; and when her former master had seated himself in the open carriage, she walked towards it, intending to place herself and child in the rear, and go with him. But, ere she reached the vehicle, she says that God revealed himself to her, with all the suddenness of a flash of lightning, showing her, in the twinkling of an eye, that he was *all over*, that he pervaded the universe, and that there was no place where God was not.

She became instantly conscious of her great sin in forgetting her almighty Friend and ever-present help in time of trouble. All her unfulfilled promises arose before her, like a vexed sea whose waves run mountains high; and her soul, which seemed but one mass of lies, shrunk back aghast from 'awful look' of Him whom she had formerly talked to, as if he had been a being like herself; and she would now fain to hide herself in the bowels of the earth, to have escaped his dread presence. But she plainly saw there was no place, not even in hell, where he was not: and where could she flee? Another such a look, as she expressed it, and she felt that she must be extinguished forever, even as one, with the breath of his mouth, blow, out a lamp, so that no spark remains.

A dire dread of annihilation now seized her, and she waited to see if, by another look, she was to be stricken from existence, swallowed up.

When at last the second look came not, and her attention was once more called to outward things, she observed her master had left and exclaiming aloud, "Oh, God, I did not know you were so big," walked into the house, and made an effort to resume her work. But the workings of the inward man were too absorbing to admit of much attention to her avocations. She desired to talk to God, but her vileness utterly forbade it, and she was not able to prefer a petition. "What!" said she, "shall I lie again to God? I have told him nothing but lies; and shall I speak again, and tell another lie to God?"

She could not; and now she began to wish for someone to speak to God for her. Then a space seemed to open between her and God, and she felt that if someone, who was worthy in the sight of heaven, would but plead *for* her in their own name, and not let God know it came from *her,* who was so unworthy, God might grant it. At length a friend appeared to stand between herself and an insulted Deity; and she felt as sensibly refreshed as when on a hot day, an umbrella had been interposed between her scorching head and a burning sun. But who was this friend? became the next inquiry. Was it Deencia, who had so often befriended her? She looked at her with her new power of sight and, lo! she, too, seemed all bruises and putrifying sores, like herself. No, it was someone very dIfferent from Deencia.

"Who are you?" she exclaimed, as the vision brightened into a form distinct, beaming with the beauty of holiness, and radiant with love. She then said, audibly addressing the mysterious visitant, "I *know* you, and I *don't* know you." Meaning, 'You seem perfectly familiar; I feel that you not only love me, but that you always have loved me, yet I know you not, I cannot call you by name'. When she said, "I know you," the subject of the vision remained distinct and quiet. When she said, "I don't know you," it moved restlessly about, like agitated waters. So while she repeated, without intermission, "I know you, I know you," that the vision might remain, "Who are you?" was the cry of her heart, and her whole soul was in one deep prayer that this heavenly personage might be revealed to her, and remain with her. At length, after bending both soul and body with the intensity of this desire, till breath and strength seemed failing, and she could maintain her position no longer, an answer came to her, saying distinctly, "It is Jesus." "Yes," she responded; "it is Jesus."

Previous to these exercises of mind, she heard Jesus mentioned in reading or speaking, but had received from what she heard no impression that he was any other than an eminent man, like a Washington or a Lafayette. Now he appeared to her delighted mental vision as so mild, so good, and so every way lovely, and he loved her so much! And, how strange that he had always loved her, and she never known it! And how great a blessing he conferred, in that he should stand between her and God! God was no longer a terror and a dread to her.

She stopped not to argue the point, even in her own mind, whether he had reconciled her to God, or God to herself, (though she thinks the former now,) being but too happy that God was no longer to her as a consuming fire, and Jesus was "altogether lovely." Her heart was now full of joy and gladness. as it had been of terror, and at one time of despair. In the light of her great happiness, the world was clad in new beauty, the very air sparkled as with diamonds, and was redolent of heaven She contemplated the unapproachable barriers that exist ed between herself and the great of this world, as the world calls greatness, and made surprising comparison between them, and the union existing between herself and Jesus, Jesus, the transcendently lovely as well as great and powerful; for so he appeared to her, though he seemed but human; and she watched for his bodily appearance feeling that she should know him, if she saw him; and when he came, she should go and dwell with him, as with a dear friend.

It was not given her to see that he loved any other; and she thought if others came to know and love him, as she did, she should be thrust aside and forgotten, being herself but a poor ignorant slave, with little to recommend her to his notice. And when she heard him spoken of, she said mentally, "What! Others know Jesus! I thought no one knew Jesus but me " and she felt a sort of jealousy, lest she should be robbed of her newly found treasure.

She conceived, one day, as she listened to reading, that she heard an intimation that Jesus was married, and hastily inquired if Jesus had a wife. 'What!' said the reader, '*God* has a wife?'

"Is Jesus *God?*" inquired Isabella.

"Yes, to be sure he is," was the answer returned. From this time, her conceptions of Jesus became more elevated and.spiritual; and she sometimes spoke of him as God, in accordance with the teaching she had received.

But when she was simply told, that the Christian world was much divided on the subject of Christ's nature some believing him to be coequal with the Father, to be God in and of himself, 'very God, of very God ;', some, that he is the well-beloved, only begotten Son of God; and others, that he is, or was, rather, but a mere man, she said, "Of that I only know as I saw. I did not see him to be God; else, how could he stand between me and God? I saw him as a friend, standing between me and God, through whom, love flowed as from a fountain."

Now, as far from expressing her views of Christ's character and office in accordance with any system of theology extant, she says she believes Jesus is the same spirit that was in our first parents, Adam and Eve, in the beginning, when they came from the hand of their Creator. When they sinned through disobedience, this pure spirit forsook them, and fled to heaven; that there it remained, until it returned again in the person of Jesus; and that, previous to a personal union with him, man is but a brute, possessing only the spirit of an animal.

She avers that, in her darkest hours, she had no fear of any worse hell than the one she then carried in her bosom; though it had ever been pictured to her in its deepest colors, and threatened her as a reward for all her misdemeanors. Her vileness and God's holiness and all pervading presence, which filled immensity, and threatened her with instant annihilation, composed the burden of her terror. Her faith in prayer is equal to her faith in the love of Jesus. Her language is, "Let others say what they will of the efficacy of prayer, Thank God! Yes *I shall always pray*," she exclaims, putting her hands together with the greatest enthusiasm.

For some time subsequent to the happy change we have spoken of, Isabella's prayers partook largely of their former character; and while, in deep affliction,she labored for the recovery of her son, she prayed with constancy and fervor; and the following may be taken as a specimen:

"Oh, God, you know how much I am distressed, for I have told you again and again. Now, God, help me get my son. If you were in trouble, as I am, and I could help you, as you can me, think I wouldn't do it? Yes, God, you know I would do it. Oh, God, you know I have no money, but you can make the people do for me, and you must make the people do for me. I will never give you peace till you do, God. Oh God, make the people hear me, don't let them turn me off, without hearing and helping me." And she has not a particle of doubt, that God heard her, and especially disposed the hearts of thoughtless clerks, eminent lawyers and grave judges and others, between whom and herself there seemed to her almost an infinite remove, to listen to her suit with patient and respectful attention, backing it up with all needed aid. The sense of her nothingness in the eyes of those with whom she contended for rights, sometimes fell on her like a heavy weight, which nothing but her unwavering confidence in an arm which she believed to be stronger than all others combined could have raised from her sinking spirit.

"Oh, how little I did feel," she repeated, with a powerful emphasis. "Neither would you wonder, if you could have seen in my ignorance and destitution, trotting about the streets meanly clad, bare-headed, and bare-footed! Oh, God only could have made such people hear me; and he did it in answer to my prayers." And this perfect trust, based on the rock of Deity, was a soul-protecting fortress; which, raising her above the battlements of fear, and shielding her from the machinations of the enemy, impelled her onward in the struggle, till the foe was vanquished, and the victory gained.

We have now seen Isabella, her youngest daughter, and her only son, in possession of, at least, their nominal freedom. It has been said that the freedom of the most free of the colored people of this country is but nominal; but stinted and limited as it is, at best, it is an *immense* remove from chattel slavery. This fact is disputed, I know; but I have no confidence in the honesty of such questionings. If they are made in sincerity, I honor not the judgment that thus decides.

Her husband, quite advanced in age, and infirm of health, was emancipated, with the balance of the adult slaves of the State, according to law, the following summer, July 4, 1828.

For a few years after this event, he was able to earn a scanty living, and when he failed to do that, he was dependent on the world's cold charity, and died in a poor house Isabella had herself and two children to provide for; her wages were trifling, for at that time the wages of females were at a small advance from nothing;

and she doubtless had to learn the first elements of economy, for what slaves, that were never allowed to make any stipulations or calculations for themselves, ever possessed an adequate idea of the true value of time, or, in fact, of any material thing in the universe? To such, prudent using is meanness, and 'saving' is a word to be sneered at. Of course, it was not in her power to make to herself a home, around whose sacred hearthstone emerged from their prison-house of bondage; a home, where she could cultivate their affection, administer to their wants, and instill into the opening minds of her children those principles of virtue, and that love of purity truth and benevolence, which must ever form the foundation of a life of usefulness and happiness. Now all this was far beyond her power or means, in more senses than one; and it should be taken into the account, whenever a comparison is instituted between the progress made by her children in virtue and goodness, and the progress of those who have been nurtured in the genial warmth of a sunny home, where good influences cluster, and bad ones are carefully excluded where line upon line, and precept upon precept are daily brought to their custodian tasks; and where, in short, every appliance is brought in requisition, that self-denying parents bring to bear on one of the dearest objects of a parents life, the

promotion of the welfare of their children. But God
forbid that this suggestion should be wrested from its
original intent, and made to shield anyone from rebuke!
Isabella's children are now of an age to know good from
evil, and may easily inform themselves on and point
where they may yet be in doubt; and if they now offer
themselves to be drawn by temptation into the path of
the destroyer or forget what is due to the mother who
has done and suffered so much for them, and who, now
that she is descending into the vale of years, and her
health and strength declining, will turn her expecting
eyes to them for aid and comfort, just as instinctively as
the child turns its confiding eye to its fond parent when
it seeks succor or for sympathy (for it is now their turn
to do the work, and bear the burdens of life, as all must
bear them in turn, as the wheel of life rolls on) if, I say
they forget this, their duty and their happiness, and
pursue an opposite course of sin and folly, they must
lose the respect of the wise and good, and find, when
too late, that 'the way of the transgressor is hard'.

A rumor was immediately circulated that Sojourner was an impostor; that she was, indeed, a man disguised in women's clothing. It appears, too, from what has since transpired, that they suspected her to be a mercenary hireling of the Republican party. "At her third appointed meeting in this vicinity, which was held in the meeting-house of the United Brethren, a large number of democrats and other pro-slavery persons were present. At the close of the meeting, Dr. T. W. Strain, the mouthpiece of the slave Democracy, requested the large congregation to hold on, and stated that a doubt existed in the minds of many persons present respecting the sex of the speaker, and that it was his impression that a majority of them believed the speaker to be a man. The doctor also affirmed (which was not believed by the friends of the slave) that it was for the speaker's special benefit that he now demanded that Sojourner submit her breast to the inspection of some of the ladies present, that the doubt might be removed by their testimony. There were a large number of ladies present, who appeared to be ashamed and indignant at such a proposition.

Sojourner's friends, some of whom had not heard the rumor, were surprised and indignant at such surmises and treatment. Confusion and uproar ensued, which was soon suppressed by Sojourner, who, immediately rising, asked them why they suspected her to be a man. The Democracy answered, 'Your voice is not the voice of a woman, it is the voice of a man, and we believe you are a man.'

Dr. Strain called for a vote, and a boisterous 'Aye,' was the result. A negative vote was not called for. Sojourner told them that her breasts had suckled many a white baby to the exclusion of her own offspring; that some of those white babies had grown to man's estate; that, although they had sucked her colored breasts, they were, in her estimation, far more manly than her persecutor appeared to be; and she quietly asked them, as she disrobed her bosom, if they, too, wished to suck! In vindication of her truthfulness, she told them that she would show her breast to the whole congregation; that it was not to her shame that she uncovered her breast before them, but to their shame. Two young men stepped forward while Sojourner exposed her naked breast to the audience. I heard a democrat say, as we were returning home from meeting, that Dr. Strain had, previous to the examination, offered to bet forty dollars that Sojourner was a man! So much for the physiological acumen of a western physician.

The reader will pardon this passing homily, while we

return to our narrative.

We were saying that the daydreams of Isabella and her husband the plan they drew of what they would do, and the comforts they thought to have, when they should obtain their freedom, and a little home of their own had all turned to thin air, by the postponement of their freedom to so late a day. These delusive hopes were never to be realized, and a new set of trials was gradually to open before her These were the heart-rending trials of watching over her children, scattered, and imminently exposed to the temptations of the adversary, with few, if any, fixed principles to sustain them.

"Oh," she says, "how little did I know myself of the best way to instruct and counsel them. Yet I did the best I knew, when with them. I took them to the religious teachings; I talked to, and prayed for and with them; when they did wrong, I scolded at and whipped them."

Isabella and her son had been free about a year, when they went to reside in the city of New York; a place which she would doubtless have avoided, could she have seen what was there in store for her; for this view into the future would have taught her what she only learned by bitter experience, that the baneful influences going up from such a city were not the best helps to education, commenced as the education of her children had been.

Peter was, at the time of which we are speaking, just at that age when no lad should be subjected to the temptations of such a place, unprotected as he was, save by the feeble arm of a mother, herself a servant there. He was growing up to be a tall, well-formed, attentive lad of quick perceptions, mild and cheerful in his disposition, with much that was open and generous about him, but with little power to withstand temptation and a ready ingenuity to provide himself with ways and means to carry out his plans, and conceal from his mother and her friends, all such as he knew would not meet their approbation. As will be readily believed, he was drawn into a circle of associates who did not improve either his habits or his morals.

Two years passed before Isabella knew what character Peter was establishing for himself among his low and worthless comrades passing under the assumed name of Peter Williams; and she began to feel a parent's pride at the promising appearance of her only son. Alas, pride and pleasure were shortly dissipated as distressing facts relative to him came one by one to her astonished ear A friend of Isabella's, a lady who was much pleased with the good humor, ingenuity, and open confessions of Peter when driven into a corner, and who, she said, was so smart, "he ought to have an education, if anyone ought," paid ten dollars, as tuition fee, for him to attend a school. But Peter, little inclined to spend his leisure hours in study, when he might be enjoying himself in the dance, or otherwise, with his boon companions, went early and made some plausible excuses to the teacher who received them as genuine, along with the ten dollars, and while his mother and her friend believed him to be improving at school, he was, proving himself in a very different place and with opposite principles.

They also procured him an excellent place as a coachman. But, wanting money, he sold his livery, and other things belonging to his master; who, having conceived a kind regard for him, considered his youth, and prevented the law from falling with all its rigor, upon his head. Still he continued to abuse his privileges, and to involve himself in repeated difficulties, from which his mother as often extricated him. At each time, she talked much and reasoned and remonstrated with him; and he would, with such perfect frankness, lay open his whole soul to her, telling her he had never intended doing harm; how he had been led along, little by little, till, before he was aware, he found himself in trouble; how he had tried to be good and how, when he would have been so, evil was present with him, indeed he knew not how it was.

His mother, beginning to feel that the city was no place for him, urged his going to sea, and would have shipped him on board a man-of-war; but Peter was not disposed to consent to that proposition while the city and its pleasures were accessible to him.

Isabella now became a prey to distressing years, dreading lest the next day or hour came fraught with the report of some dreadful crime, committed or abetted by her son. She thanks the Lord for sparing her that giant sorrow, as all his wrongdoings never ranked higher, in the eye of the law, than misdemeanours. But as she could see no improvement in Peter, as a last resort, she resolved to leave him, unassisted, to bear the penalty of his conduct, and see what effect that would have on him. In the trial hour, she remained firm in her resolution.

Peter again fell into the hands of the police, and sent for his mother, as usual; but she went not to his relief. In his extremity, he sent for Peter Williams, a respectable colored barber, whose name he had been wearing, and who sometimes helped young culprits out of their troubles, and sent them from city dangers, by shipping them on board of whaling vessels.

The curiosity of this man was awakened by the culprit's bearing his own name. He went to the Tombs and inquired into his case, but could not believe what

Peter told him respecting his mother and family. Yet he redeemed him, and Peter promised to leave New York in a vessel that was to sail in the course of a week.

He went to see his mother, and informed her of what had happened to him. She listened incredulously, as to an idle tale. He asked her to go with him and see for herself. She went, giving no credence to his story till she found herself in the presence of Mr. Williams, and heard him saying to her, "I am very glad I have assisted your son. He stood in great need of sympathy and assistance, but I could not think he had such a mother here, although he assured me he had."

Isabella's great trouble now was, a fear lest her son should deceive his benefactor, and be missing when the vessel sailed; but he begged her earnestly to trust in him for he said he had resolved to do better and meant to abide by the resolve. Isabella's heart gave her no peace till the time of sailing, when Peter sent Mr. Williams and another messenger whom she knew, to tell her he had sailed. But for a month afterwards, she expected to see him emerging from some by-place in the city, appearing before her; so afraid was she that he was still unfaithful, and doing wrong. But he did not appear, and at length she believed he had really gone.

He left in summer of 1839, and his friends heard nothing from him till his mother received the following, dated October 17 1840:

My dear and beloved mother,

I take this opportunity to write to you and inform you that I am well, and in hopes for to find you the same. I am got on board the same unlucky ship Done, of Nantucket I am sorry for to say, that I have been punished once severely, by shoving my head in the fire for other folks. We have had bad luck, but in hopes to have better. We have about 230 on board.

I would like to know how my sisters are. Does my cousin live in New York yet? Have you got my letter? If not, inquire to Mr. Pierce Whiting's.

I wish you would write me an answer as soon as possible. I am your only son, that is so far from your home, in the wide, briny ocean. I have seen more of the world than ever I expected, and if I ever should return home safe, I will tell you all my troubles and hardships.

Mother, I hope you do not forget me, your dear and only son. I should like to know about Sophia, Betsey and Hannah. I hope you all will forgive me for all that I have done.

Your son, PETER VAN WAGENER

Another letter reads as follows, dated March 22:

My dear beloved mother,

I take this opportunity to write to you, and inform you

that I have been well and in good health. I have wrote a letter
before, but have received no answer and was very anxious to
see you. I hope that it will be a short time. I have had very
hard luck, but hope to have better in time to come. I should
like if my sisters are well, and all the people round the
neighborhood. I expect to be home in twenty months or
thereabouts. I have seen Samuel Laterett. Beware! There has
happened very bad news to tell you, that Peter Jackson is
dead. He died within two days' sail of Otaheite, one of the
Society Islands. The Peter Jackson that used to live at
Laterett's; he died on board the ship Done, of Nantucket,
Captain Miller, in the latitude 15 53, and longitude 148 30
W.

Notice, when this you see, remember me, and place me in
your mind:

Get me to my home, in the far distant west
To the scenes of my childhood, that I like best
Where tall cedars grow, and bright waters
flow
Where my parents will greet me, white man,
let me go.

Let me go to the spot where the cateract plays
Where oft I have sported in my boyish days
And there is my poor mother, whose heart

ever flows
At the sight of her poor child, to her let me go
Let me go.

I have no more to say at present, but write as soon as possible.
Your only son

Another, containing the last intelligence she has had from her son, reads as follows, and was dated Sept. 19, 1841.

Dear mother,

I take this opportunity to write to you and inform you that I am well and in good health, and in hope to find you the same. This is the fifth letter that I have wrote to you, and have received no answer, and it makes me very uneasy. So pray write as quick as you can. Tell me how all the people is about the neighbourhood.

We are out from home twenty-three months and hopes to be home in fifteen months. I have not much to say; but tell me if you have been up home since I left or not. I want to know what sort of a time is at home.

We had very bad luck when we first came out, but recently we have had very good; so I am in hopes to do well, but if I don't do well, you need not expect me home in five years. So write as quick as you can, won't you. Now I am going to put an end to my writing.

    Your only son.

Since the date of the last letter, Isabella has heard no
tidings from her long-absent son, though ardently does
her mother's heart long for such tidings, as her thoughts
follow him around the world, in his perilous vocation,
saying within herself 'He is good now, I have no doubt;
I feel sure that he has persevered, and kept the resolve
be made before he left home;he seemed so different
before he went, so determined to do better. His letters
are inserted here for preservation, in ease they prove the
last she ever hears from him in this world.

"At all of our meetings we have been told that armed men were in our midst and had declared they would blow out our brains. I carry no weapon; the Lord will preserve me without weapons. I feel safe here in the midst of my enemies; for the truth is powerful and will prevail.

Cannonballs may aid the truth, but thought's a stronger weapon. Slavery has made a conquest in this country by the suppression of free speech, and freedom must make a conquest by the steadfast support of free speech."

When Isabella had obtained the freedom of her son, she remained in Kingston, where she had been drawn by the judicial process about a year, during which time she became a member of the Methodist Church there: and when she went to New York, she took a letter missive from that church to the Methodist Church in John Street.

Afterwards, she withdrew her connection with that church, and joined Zion Church in Church Street, composed entirely of colored people. With the latter church she remained until she went to reside with Mr. Pierson after which, she was gradually drawn into the 'kingdom' set up by the prophet Matthias, in the name of God the Father; for he said the spirit of God the Father dwelt in him.

While Isabella was in New York, her sister Sophia came from Newburg to reside in the former place. Isabella had been favored with occasional interviews with this sister, although at one time she lost sight of her for the space of seventeen years almost the entire period of her being at Mr. Dumont's and when she appeared before her again, handsomely dressed, she did not recognize her, till informed who she was. Sophia informed her that her brother Michael (a brother she had never seen) was in the city; and when she introduced him to Isabella, he informed her that their sister Nancy had been living in the city, and had deceased a few months before. He described her features, her dress, her manners, said she had for some time been a member in Zion Church, naming the class she belonged to.

Almost instantly Isabella recognized her as a sister in the church with whom she had knelt at the altar, and with whom she had exchanged the speaking pressure of the hand in recognition of their spiritual sisterhood; little thinking at the time, that they were also children of the same earthly parents, Bomefree and Mau-mau Bett. As inquiries and answers rapidly passed, and the conviction deepened that this was their sister, the very sister they had heard so much of, but had never seen (for she was the self-same sister that had been locked in the great old fashioned sleigh-box, when she was taken away, never to behold her mother's face again this side of the spirit-land, and Michael the narrator, was the brother who had shared her fate). Isabella thought, 'Damn! Here she was; we met; and was I not, at the time, struck with the peculiar feeling of her hand, the bony hardness so just like mine, and yet I could not know she was my sister; and now I see she looked so like my mother."

And Isabella wept, and not alone; Sophia wept, and the strong man, Michael, mingled his tears with theirs.

"Oh Lord," inquired Isabella, "what is this slavery, that it can do such dreadful things? What evil can it not do?"

Well may she ask, for surely the evils it can and does do daily and hourly can never be summed up, till we can see them as they are recorded by him who writes no errors, and reckons without mistake. This account, which now varies so widely in the estimate of different minds, will be viewed alike by all.

Think you, dear reader, when that day comes, the

most rabid abolitionist will say "Behold, I saw all this whilst on the earth?" Will he not rather say, "Oh, who has conceived the breadth and depth of this moral malaria, this putrescent plague-spot?" Perhaps the pioneers in the slaves cause will be as much surprised as any to find that with all their looking, there remained so much unseen.

There are some hard things that crossed Isabella's life while in slavery that she has no desire to publish, for various reasons. First because the parties from whose hands she suffered them have rendered up their account to a higher tribunal, and their innocent friends alone are living, to have their feelings injured by the recital; secondly, because they are not all for the public ear, by their very nature; thirdly, and not least, because, she says, were she to tell all that happened to her as a slave all that she knows is 'God's truth', it would seem to others, especially the uninitiated, so unaccountable, so unreasonable, and what is usually called so unnatural (though it may be questioned whether people do not always act naturally), they would not easily believe it.

"Why, no," she says, "they'd call me a liar. They would indeed, and I do not wish to say anything to destroy my own character for veracity, though what I say is strictly true."

Some things have been omitted through forgetfulness, which not having been mentioned in their place can only be briefly spoken of here; such as, that her father Bomefree had had two wives before he took Mau-mau Bett; one of whom, if not both, were torn from him by the iron hand of the ruthless trafficker in human flesh; that her husband Thomas, after one of his wives had been sold away from him, ran away to New York, where he remained a year or two, before he was recovered and taken back to the prison-house of slavery; that her master Dumont, when he promised Isabella one year of her time, before the State should make her free, made the same promise to her husband, and in addition to freedom, they were promised a log cabin home of their own; all of which, with the one thousand and one daydreams resulting therefrom, went into the depository of unfulfilled promises and unrealized hopes; that she had often heard her father repeat a story of a little slave child which, because it annoyed family with its cries, was lifted up by a white man who dashed its brains out against the wall. An Indian (for Indians were plenty in that region then) passed along as the bereaved mother washed the bloody corpse of her murdered child, and learning the cause of its death, said, with characteristic vehemence,

"If I had been here, I would have put my tomahawk in the murderer's head!"

Of the cruelty of one Hasbrouck. He had a sick slave woman, who was lingering with a slow consumption, whom he made to spin, regardless of her weakness and suffering; and this woman had a child, that was unable to walk or talk, at the age of five years, neither could it cry like other children, but made a constant, piteous, moaning sound. This exhibition of helplessness and imbecility, instead of exciting the master's pity, stung his cupidity, and so enraged him, that he would kick the poor thing about like a football.

Isabella's informant had seen this brute of a man, when the child was curled up under a chair, innocently amusing itself with a few sticks, drag it thence, that he might have the pleasure of tormenting it. She had seen him, with one kick, send it rolling quite across the room, and in down the steps to the door. Oh, how she wished the child might instantly die, "But," she said "it seemed as tough as a moccasin."

Though it *did* die at last, and made glad the heart of its friends; and its persecutor, no doubt, rejoiced with them, but from very different motives. But the day of retribution was not far off, for he sickened, and his reason fled. It was fearfull to hear his old slave soon tell how, in the day of his calamity, she treated *him*.

She was very strong and therefore selected to support her master, as he sat up in bed, by putting her arms around, while she stood behind him. It was then that she did her best to wreak her vengeance on him. She would clutch his feeble frame in her iron grasp, as in a vice and, when her mistress did not see, would give him a squeeze, a shake, and lifting him up, set him down as hard as possible. If his breathing betrayed too tight a grasp, and her mistress said, "Be careful, don't hurt him, Soan," her ever-ready answer was, "Oh no, Missus, no," in her most pleasant tone and then, as soon as Missus' eyes and ears were engaged away, another grasp, another shake, another bounce. She was afraid the disease alone would let him recover, an event she dreaded more than to do wrong herself. Isabella asked her, if she were afraid his spirit would haunt her. "Oh, no," says Soan, "he was so wicked, the devil will never let him out of hell long enough for that."

Many slaveholders boast of the love of their slaves. How would it freeze the blood of some of them to know what kind of love rankles in the bosoms of slaves for them. Witness the attempt to poison Mrs. Calhoun, and hundreds of similar cases. Most surprising to everybody, because committed by slaves supposed to be 'grateful' for their chains.

These reflections bring to mind a discussion on the

point between the writer and a slaveholding friend from Kentucky, on Christmas morning, 1846. We had asserted, that until mankind were far in advance of what they now are, irresponsible power over our fellow-beings would be, as it is, abused. Our friend declared it his conviction, that the cruelties of slavery existed chiefly in imagination, and that people in Kentucky were above ill-treating a helplesss slave. We answered, that if his belief was well-founded, the people in Kentucky were greatly in advance of the people in the rest of the country. No, we would not answer for our own conduct even on so delicate a point.

The next evening, he very magnanimously overthrew his own position and established ours, by informing us that, on the morning previous, and as near as we could learn, at the very hour in which we were earnestly discussing the probabilities of the case, a young woman of fine appearance, and high standing in society, the pride of her husband, and the mother of an infant daughter, only a few miles from us was actually beating in the skull of a slave-woman called Tabby; and not content with that, had her tied up and whipped, after her skull was broken, and she died hanging to the bedstead, to which she had been fastened. When informed that Tabby was dead, she answered, "I am glad of it, for she has worried my life out of me." But

Tabby's highest good was probably not the end proposed by her mistress, for no one supposed she meant to kill her. Tabby was considered quite lacking in good sense, and no doubt belonged to that class in the South that are silly enough to die of 'moderate correction'.

A mob collected around the house for an hour or two, in that manner expressing a momentary indignation. But was she treated as a murderess? Not at all. She was allowed to take boat (for her residence was near the beautiful Ohio) that evening, to spend a few months with her absent friends, after which she returned and remained with her husband, no one to 'molest or make her afraid'.

Had she been left to the punishment of an outraged conscience from right motives, I would have rejoiced with joy. But to see the life of one woman, and she a murderess, put in the balance against the lives of three millions of innocent slaves, and to contrast her punishment with what I felt would be the punishment of one who was merely suspected of being an equal friend of all mankind, regardless of color or condition, caused my blood to stir within me, and my heart to sicken at the thought. Her husband was absent from home, at the time alluded to; and when he arrived, some weeks afterwards, bringing beautiful presents to his cherished companion, he beheld his once happy home deserted, Tabby murdered and buried in the garden and the wife of his bosom, and the mother of his child, the doer of the dreadful deed, a murderess!

When Isabella went to New York City, she went in company with a Miss Grear, who introduced her to the family of Mr. James Latourette, a wealthy merchant, and a Methodist in religion, but who, the latter part of his life, felt that he had outgrown ordinances, and advocated free meetings, holding them at his own dwelling-house for several years previous to his death. She worked for them, and they generously gave her a home while she labored for others, and in their kindness made her as one of their own.

At that time, the 'moral reform' movement awakening the attention of the benevolent in that city. Many women, among whom were Mrs. Latourette and Miss Grear, became deeply interested in making an attempt to reform their fallen sisters, even the most degraded of them; and in this enterprise of labor and danger, they enlisted Isabella and others, who for a time put forth their most zealous efforts, and performed the work of missionaries with much apparent success. Isabella accompanied those ladies to the most wretched abodes of vice and misery, and sometimes she went where they dared not follow. They even succeeded in establishing prayer meetings in several places, where such a thing might least have been expected.

But these meetings soon became the most noisy, shouting, ranting and boisterous of gatherings; where they became delirious with excitement, and then exhausted from over-action. Such meetings Isabella had not much sympathy with, at best. But one evening she attended one of them, where the members of it, in a fit of ecstasy, jumped upon her cloak in such a manner as to drag her to the floor and then, thinking she had fallen in a spiritual trance, they increased their glorifications on her account, jumping, shouting stamping, and clapping of hands; rejoicing so much over her spirit, and so entirely over her body, that she suffered much, both from fear and bruises, and . ever after refused to attend any more such meetings, doubting much whether God had any thing to do with such worship

I'm awful hard on dress, you know. Women, you forget that you are the mothers of creation, you forget your sons were cut off like grass by the war, and the land was covered with their blood; you rig yourselves up in panniers and Grecian-bend backs and flummeries; yes, and mothers and gray-haired grandmothers wear high-heeled shoes and humps on their heads, and put them on their babies, and stuff them out so that they keel over when the wind blows.

O mothers, I'm ashamed of you. What will such lives as you live do for humanity? When I saw those women on the stage at the Woman's Suffrage Convention the other day, I thought, what kind of reformers be you, with goose-wings on your heads, as if you were going to fly, and dressed in such ridiculous fashion, talking about reform and women's rights. 'Pears to me, you had better reform yourselves first.

Some women wear two heads on their shoulders with but little if any brains in either. I knew a young woman who had her hair cut on account of an impotency in her head and eyes. When the hair was cut, she weaved extra hair in, put it into a

*net and and wore it for the night. Her hair grew again but
still she continued to wear the extra hair. Perhaps there is no
truer saying than that folly is a fund that will never lose
ground while fools are so rife in the nation.*

We now come to an eventful period in the life of
Isabella, as identified with one of the most
extraordinary religious delusions of modern times; but
the limits prescribed for the present work forbid a
minute narration of all the occurrences that transpired
in relation to it

After she had joined the African Church in Church,
and during her membership there, she frequently
attended Mr. Latourette's meetings, at one of which, Mr.
Smith invited her to go to a prayer meeting, or to
instruct the girls at the Magdalene Asylum, Bowery
Hill, then under the protection of Mr. Pierson, and some
other persons, chiefly respectable females. To reach the
Asylum, Isabella called on Katy, Mr. Pierson's colored
servant, of whom she had some knowledge. Mr. Pierson
saw her there, conversed with her, asked her if she had
been baptized, and was answered, characteristically,
"By the Holy Ghost." After this, Isabella saw Katy
several times, and occasionally Mr. Pierson, who
engaged her to keep the house while Katy went to
Virginia to see her children. This engagement was

considered an answer to prayer by Mr. Pierson, who had both fasted and prayed on the subject, while Katy and Isabella appeared to see in it the hand of God.

Mr. Pierson was characterized by a strong devotional spirit, which finally became highly fanatical. He assumed the title of Prophet, asserting that God had called him in an omnibus, in these words: 'Thou art Elijah, the Tishbite. Gather unto me all the members of Israel at the foot of Mount Carmel', which he understood as meaning the gathering of his friends at Bowery Hill. Not long afterward, he became acquainted with the notorious Matthias, whose career was as extraordinary as it was brief.

Robert Matthews, or Matthias, (as he was usually called) was of Scotch extraction, but a native of New York, and at that time about forty-seen years of age. He was religiously brought up, among the Burghers, a sect of Presbyterians; the clergyman the Rev. Mr. Bevridge, visiting the family after the manner of the church, and being pleased with Robert, put his hand on his head, when a boy, and pronounced a blessing, and this blessing, with his natural qualities, determined his character; for he ever after thought he should be a distinguished man. Matthias was brought up a farmer till nearly eighteen years of age, but acquired indirectly the art of a carpenter, without any regular apprenticeship, and showed considerable mechanical skill. He obtained property from his uncle, Robert Thompson, and then he went into business as a store-keeper, was considered respectable, and became a member of the Scotch Presbyterian Church. He married in 1813, and continued in business in Cambridge. In 1816, he ruined himself by a building speculation, and the derangement of the currency which denied bank facilities, and soon after he came to New York with his family, and worked at his trade. He afterwards removed to Albany, and became a hearer at the Dutch Reformed Church, then under Dr. Ludlow's charge. He was frequently much excited on religious subjects.

In 1829, he was well known, if not for street preaching, for loud discussions and pavement exhortations, but he did not make set sermons. In the beginning of 1830, he was only considered zealous; but in the same year he prophesied the destruction of the Albanians and their capital, and while preparing to shave, with the Bible before him, he suddenly put down the soap and exclaimed, "I've found it! I have found a text which proves that no man who shaves his beard can be a true Christian." Shortly afterwards, without shaving, he went to the Mission House to deliver an address which he had promised, and in this address he proclaimed his new character, pronounced vengeance on the land, and that the law of God was the only rule of government, and that he was commanded to take possession of the world in the name of the King of Kings. His harangue was cut short by the trustees putting out the lights. About this time, Matthias advised his wife to fly with him from the destruction which awaited them in the city; and on her refusal, partly on account of Matthias calling himself a Jew, whom she was unwilling to retain as a husband, he left her, taking some of the children to his sister in Argyle, forty miles from Albany. At Argyle he entered the church and interrupted the minister, declaring the congregation in darkness, and warning them to repentance He was, of course, taken out of the church, and as he was advertised in the Albany papers, he was sent back to his family. His beard had now obtained a respectable length, and thus he attracted attention, and easily obtained an audience in the streets. For this he was sometimes arrested, once by mistake for Adam Paine, who collected the crowd, and then left Matthias with it on the approach of the officers. He repeatedly urged his wife to accompany him on a mission to convert the world, declaring that food could be obtained from the roots of the forest, if not administered otherwise. At this time he assumed the name of Matthias, called himself a Jew, set out on a mission, taking a western course, and visiting a brother at Rochester, a skilful mechanic, since dead. Leaving his brother, he proceeded on his mission over the Northern States, occasionally returning to Albany.

After visiting Washington, and passing through Pennsylvania, he came to New York. His appearance at the time was mean, but grotesque, and his sentiments but little known.

On May the 5th, 1832, he first called on Mr. Pierson in Fourth street, in his absence. Isabella was alone in the house in which she had lived since the previous autumn. On opening the door, she, for the first time; beheld Matthias, and her early impression of seeing Jesus in the flesh rushed into her mind. She heard his injury and invited him into the parlor; and being naturally curious, and much excited, and possessing a good deal of tact, she drew him into conversation, stated her own opinions, and heard his replies and explanations. Her faith was at first staggered by his declaring himself a Jew; but on this point she was relieved by his saying, "Do you not remember how Jesus prayed?" and repeated part of the Lord's prayer, in proof that the Father's kingdom was to come, and not the Son's. She then understood him to be a converted Jew, and in the conclusion she says she "felt as if God had sent him to set up the kingdom." Thus Matthias at

once secured the good will of Isabella, and we may
suppose obtained from her some information in relation
to Mr. Pierson, especially that Mrs. Pierson declared
there was no true church, and approved of Mr. Pierson's
preaching. Matthias left the house, promising to return
on Saturday evening. Mr. P. at this time had not seen
Matthias.

Isabella, desirous of hearing the expected
conversation between Matthias and Mr. Pierson on
Saturday, hurried her work, got it finished, and was
permitted to be present. Indeed, the sameness of belief
made her familiar with her employer, while her
attention to her work, and characteristic faithfulness,
increased his confidence. This intimacy, the result of
holding the same faith, and the principle afterwards
adopted of having but one table, and all things in
common made her at once the domestic and the equal
and the depository of very curious, if not valuable
information. To this object, even her color assisted.
Persons who have travelled in the South know the
manner in which the colored people, and especially
slaves, are treated; they are scarcely regarded as being
present. This trait in our American character has been
frequently noticed by foreign travellers. One English
lady remarks that she discovered, in course of
conversation with a Southern married gentleman, that a

colored girl slept in his bedroom, in which also was his wife; and when he saw that it occasioned some surprise, he remarked, "What would I do if I wanted a glass of water in the night?" Other travellers have remarked that the presence of colored people never seemed to interrupt conversation of any kind for one moment.

Isabella, then, was present at the first interview between Matthias and Pierson. At this interview, Mr. Pierson asked Matthias if he had a family, to which he replied in the affirmative; he asked him about his beard, and he gave a scriptural reason, asserting also that the Jews did not shave, and that Adam had a beard. Mr. Pierson detailed to Matthias his experience, and Matthias gave his, and they mutually discovered that they held the same sentiments, both admitting the direct influence of the Spirit, and the transmission of spirits from one body to another. Matthias admitted the call of Mr. Pierson which, on this occasion, he gave in these words: "Thou art Elijah the Tishbite, and thou shalt go before me. In the spirit and power of Elias, to prepare my way before me." And Mr. Pierson admitted Matthias' call, completed his declaration on the 20th of June, in Argyle, which, by a curious coincidence, was the very day which Pierson had received his call. Such singular coincidences have a powerful effect on excited minds. From that discovery, Pierson and Matthias rejoiced in each other, and became kindred spirits. Matthias, however, claiming to be the Father, or to possess the spirit of the Father — he was God upon earth, because the spirit of God dwelt in him — while Pierson then understood that his mission was like that of John the Baptist, which the name Elias meant. This conference ended with an invitation to supper, and Matthias and Pierson washing each other's feet. Mr. Pierson preached on the following Sunday, but after which, he declined in favor of Matthias, and some of the party believed that the 'kingdom' had then come.

As a specimen of Matthias' preaching and sentiments, the following is said to be reliable:

"The spirit that built the Tower of Babel is now in the world, it is the spirit of the devil. The spirit of man never goes upon the clouds; all who think so are Babylonians The only heaven is on the earth All who are ignorant of truth are Ninevites. The Jews did not crucify Christ, it was the Gentiles. Every Jew has his guardian angel attending him in this world. God don't speak through preachers; he speaks through me, his prophet.

"John the Baptist," (addressing Mr. Pierson) "read the tenth chapter of Revelations..."

After the reading of the chapter, the prophet resumed speaking, as follows:

"Ours is the mustard seed kingdom which is to

spread all over the earth. Our creed is truth, and no man can truth unless he obeys John the Baptist. and comes clean into the church.

"All *real* men will be saved; all mock men will be damned. When a person has the Holy Ghost, then he is a man, and not till then. They who teach women are of the wicked. The communion is all nonsense; so is prayer. Eating a nip of bread and drinking a little wine won't do any good. All who admit members into their church, and suffer them to hold their lands and houses, their sentence is, 'Depart ye wicked, I know you not'. All females who lecture their husbands, their sentence is the same. The sons of truth are to enjoy all the good things of this world, and must use their means to bring it about. Everything that has the smell of woman will be destroyed. Woman is the capsheaf of the abomination of desolation full of all devilry. In a short time the world will take fire and dissolve; it is combustible already. All women, not obedient, had better become so as soon as possible, and let the wicked spirit depart and become temples of truth. Praying is as mocking. When you see any one wring the neck of a fowl, instead of cutting of its head, he has not got the Holy Ghost (cutting gives the least pain).

"All who eat swine's flesh are of the devil; and just as certain as he eats it, he will tell a lie in less than half an hour. If you eat a piece of pork, it will go crooked through you, and the Holy Ghost will not stay in you but one or the other must leave the house pretty soon. The pork will be as crooked in you as rams' horns, and as great a nuisance as the hogs in the street.

"The cholera is not the right word; it is choler, which means God's wrath. Abraham, Isaac, and Jacob are not in this world; they did not go up in the clouds as some believe, why should they go there? They don't want to go there to box the compass from one place to another. The Christians nowadays are for setting up the *Son's* kingdom. It is not his; it is the Father's kingdom. It puts me in mind of the man in the country, who took his son in business, and had his sign made, *Hitchcock & Son*, but the son wanted it *Hithcock & Father.* That is the way with your Christians. They talk of the Son's kingdom first, and not the Father's kingdom."

Matthias and his disciples at this time did not believe in a resurrection of the body, but that the spirits of the former saints would enter the bodies of the present generation, and thus begin heaven upon earth, of which he and Mr. Pierson were the first fruits.

Matthias made the residence of Mr. Pierson his own; but the latter, being apprehensive of popular violence in his house, if Matthias remained there, proposed a monthly allowance to him, and advised him to occupy another dwelling. Matthias accordingly took a house in Clarkson Street, and then sent for his family at Albany, but they declined coming to the city. However, his brother George complied with a similar offer, bringing his family with him, where they found very comfortable quarters. Isabella was employed to do the housework.

In May,1833, Matthias left his house, and placed the furniture, part of which was Isabella's, elsewhere, living himself at the hotel on the corner of Marketfield and West streets. Isabella found employment at Mr. Whiting's on Canal Street, and did the washing for Matthias by Mrs. Whiting's permission.

Of the subsequent removal of Matthias to the farm and residence of Mr. B. Folger, at Sing Sing, where he was joined by Mr. Pierson, and others laboring under a similar religious delusion; the sudden, melancholy and somewhat suspicious death of Mr. Pierson, and the arrest of Matthias on the charge of his murder, ending in a verdict of not guilty; the criminal connection that subsisted between Matthias, Mrs. Folger, and other members of the 'kingdom' as 'match-spirits'; the final dispersing of this deluded company, and the voluntary exilement of Matthias in the far West, after his release, wee do not deem it useful or necessary to give any particulars. Those who are curious to know what there transpired are referred to a work published in New York in 1835, entitled *Fanaticism: its sources and influences.* Suffice it to say, that while Isabella vas a member of the household at Sing Sing, doing much laborious service in the spirit of religious disinterestedness, and gradually getting her vision purged and her mind cured of its illusions, she happily escaped the contamination that surrounded her, assiduously endeavoring to discharge all her duties in a becoming manner.

When Isabella resided with Mr. Pierson, he was in the habit of fasting every Friday; not eating or drinking anything from Thursday evening to six o'clock on Friday evening.

Then, again, he would fast two nights and three days, neither eating nor drinking; refusing himself even a sip of cold water till the third day at night, when he took supper again, as usual.

Isabella asked him why he fasted. He answered that fasting gave him great light in the things of God; which answer gave birth to the following train of thought in the mind of Isabella: 'Well, if fasting will give light inwardly and spiritually, I need it as much as anybody and I'll fast too. If Mr. Pierson needs to fast two nights and three days, then I, who need light more than he does, ought to fast more, and I will fast three nights and three days'.

This resolution she carried out to the letter, putting not so much as a drop of water in her mouth for three whole days and nights. The fourth morning, as she arose to her feet, not having power to stand, she fell to the door; but recovering herself sufficiently, she made her way to the pantry, and feeling herself quite voracious, and fearing that she might now offend God by her voracity, compelled herself to breakfast on dry bread and water, eating a large six-penny loaf before she felt at all stayed or satisfied. She says she did get light, but it was all in her body and none in her mind and this lightness of body lasted a long time. Oh, she was so light, and felt so well, she could skim around like a gull.

The first years spent by Isabella in the city, she accumulated more than enough to supply all her wants, and she placed all the overplus in the Savings' Bank. Afterwards, while living with Mr. Pierson, he prevailed on her to take it thence, and invest it in a common fund which he was about establishing, as a fund to be drawn from by the faithful; the faithful, of course, were the handful who would subscribe to his peculiar creed. This fund, commenced by Mr. Pierson, afterwards became part and parcel of the kingdom of which Matthias assumed to be head. And at the breaking up of the kingdom, her little property was merged in the general ruin, or went to enrich those who profited by the loss of others, if any such there were.

Mr. Pierson and others had so assured her that the fund would supply all her wants, at all times, and in all emergencies, and to the end of life, that she became perfectly careless on the subject asking for no interest when she drew her money from the bank, and taking no account of the sum she placed in the fund. She recovered a few articles of furniture from the wreck of the kingdom, and received a small sum of money from Mr. B. Folger, as the price of Mrs. Folger's attempt to convict her of murder. With this to start upon, she commenced anew her labors, in the hope of yet being able to accumulate a sufficiency to make a little home for herself, in her advancing age. With this stimulus before her, she toiled hard, working early and late, doing a great deal for a little money, and turning her hand to almost anything that promised good pay. Still, she did not prosper; and somehow, could not contrive to save a single dollar for a rainy day.

When this had been the state of her affairs some time, she suddenly paused, and taking a retrospective view of what had passed, inquired within herself, why it was that, for all her unwearied labors, she had nothing to show, why it was that others, with much less care and labor, could hoard up treasures for themselves and children?

She became more and more convinced as she reasoned that everything she had undertaken in the city of New York had finally proved a failure; and where her hopes had been raised the highest, there she felt the failure had been the greatest, and the disappointment most severe.

After turning it in her mind for some time, she came to the conclusion, that she had been taking part in a great drama, which was, in itself, but one great system of robbery and wrong. "Yes," she said, "the rich rob the poor, and the poor rob one another."

True, she had not received labor from others, and stinted their pay, as had been practised against her; but she had taken their work from them, which was their only means of making money, and was the same to them in the end. For instance, a gentleman where she lived would give her a half dollar to hire a poor man to clear the new-fallen snow from the steps and sidewalks. She would arise early, and perform the labor herself putting the money into her own pocket. A poor man would come along, saying she ought to have let him have the job; he was poor, and needed the pay for his family. She would harden her heart against him, and answer "I am poor too, and I need it for mine." But, in her retrospection, she thought of all the misery she might have been adding to, in her selfish grasping, and it troubled her conscience sorely; and this insensibility to the claims of human brotherhood, and the wants of the destitute and wretched poor, she now saw, as she never had done before, to be unfeeling, selfish and wicked. These reflections and convictions gave rise to a sudden revulsion of feeling in the heart of Isabella, and she began to look upon money and property with great indifference, if not contempt, being at that time unable, probably, to discern any difference between a miserly grasping at and hoarding of money and means, and a true use of the good things of this life for one's own comfort, and the relief of such as she might be enabled to befriend and assist. One thing she was sure of, the precepts, 'Do unto others as you would that others should do unto you', 'Love your neighbour as yourself', and so forth, were maxims that had been but little thought of by herself; or practised by those about her.

Her next decision was, that she must leave the city; it was no place for her. She felt called in spirit to travel east and lecture. She had never been further east than the city, neither had she any friends there of whom she had particular reason to expect anything; yet to her it was plain that her mission lay in the east, and that she would find friends there. She determined on leaving, but these determinations and convictions she kept close locked in her own breast, knowing that if her children and friends were aware of it, they would make such an ado about it as would render it very unpleasant, if not distressing to all parties. Having made what preparations for leaving she deemed necessary, which was, to put up a few articles of clothing in a pillowcase, all else being deemed an unnecessary incumbrance, about an hour before she left, she informed Mrs Whiting, the woman of the house where she was stopping, that her name was no longer Isabella, but SOJOURNER; and that she was going east. And to her inquiry, "Why are you going east?" her answer was, "The Spirit calls me there, and I must go."

She left the city on the morning of the 1st of June 1843, crossing over to Brooklyn, L. I., and taking the rising sun for her only compass and guide, she remembered Lot's wife, and hoping to avoid her fate, she resolved not to look back till she felt sure the wicked city from which she was fleeing was left too far behind to be visible in the distance; and when she first ventured to look back, she could just discern the blue cloud of smoke that hung over it, and she thanked the Lord that she was far removed from what seemed to her a second Sodom.

She was now fairly started on her pilgrimage; bundle in one hand, and a little basket of provisions in the other, and two York shillings in her purse, her mind strong in the faith that her true work lay before her, be that the Lord was her director; and she doubted not that he would provide for and protect her, and that it would be very censurable in her to burden herself with anything more than a moderate supply for her then present needs. Her mission was not merely to travel east, but to lecture, as she designated it; testifying of the hope that was in her, exhorting the people to embrace Jesus, and refrain from sin, the nature and origin of which she explained to them in accordance with her own most curious and original views. Through her life, and all its chequered changes, she has ever clung fast to her first permanent impressions on religious subjects.

Wherever night overtook her, there she sought for free lodgings if she might, if not, she paid at a tavern, if she chanced to be at one, if not, at a private dwelling; with the rich, if they would receive her, if not, with the poor.

But she soon discovered that the largest houses were nearly always full; if not quite full, company was soon expected; and that it was much easier to find an unoccupied corner in a small house than in a large one; and if a person possessed but a miserable roof over his head, you might be sure of a welcome to part of it.

But this, she had penetration enough to see, was quite as much the effect of a want of sympathy as of benevolence; and this was also very apparent in her religious conversations with people who were strangers to her. She said she never could find out whether the rich had any religion. "If I had been rich and accomplished, I could; for the rich could always find religion in the rich, as I could find it in the poor."

At first, she attended such meetings as she heard of in the vicinity of her travels, and spoke to the people as she found them assembled. Afterwards, she advertised meetings of her own, and held forth to large audiences, having, as she says, "a good time."

When she became weary of travelling, and wished a place to stop a while and rest herself, some opportunity was always near at hand. The first time she needed rest, a man accosted her as she was walking, inquiring if she was looking for work. She told him that was not the object of her travels, but that she would willingly work a few days, if any one wanted. He requested her to go to his family, who were sadly in want of assistance, which he had been thus far unable to supply. She went to the house where she was directed. and was received by his family (one of whom was ill), as a 'God send'. When she felt constrained to resume her journey, they were very sorry, and would fain have detained her longer; but as she urged the necessity of leaving, they offered her what seemed in her eyes a great deal of money as a remuneration for her labor, and an expression of their gratitude for her opportune assistance; but she would only receive a very little of it; enough, as she says, to enable her to pay tribute to Caesar, if it was demanded of her; and two or three York shillings at a time were all she allowed herself to take; and then, with pulse replenished, and strength renewed, she would once more set out to perform her mission.

As she drew near the centre of the island, she commenced, one evening at nightfall, to solicit the favor of a night's lodging. She had repeated her request a great many, it seemed to her some twenty times, and as many times she received a negative answer. She walked on .The stars and the tiny horns of the new moon shed but a dim light on her lonely way, when she was familiarly accosted by two Indians, who took her for an acquaintance. She told them they were mistaken in the person; she was a stranger there, and asked them the direction to a tavern. They informed her it was yet a long way — some two miles or so, and inquired if she were alone. Not wishing for their protection, or knowing what might be the character of their kindness, she answered, "No, not exactly," and walked on. At the end of a weary way, she came to the tavern, or rather, to a large building, which was occupied as court-house, tavern and jail, and on asking for a night's lodging, was informed she could stay, if she would consent to be locked in. This to her mind was an insuperable objection. To have a key turned on her was a thing not to be thought of, at least not to be endured, and she again took up her line of march, preferring to walk beneath the open sky, to being locked up by a stranger in such a place. She had not walked far, before she heard the voice of a woman under an open shed. She ventured to accost her, and inquired if she knew where she could get in for the night. The woman answered that she did not, unless she went home with them; and turning to her 'good man', asked him if the stranger could not share their home for the night, to which he cheerily assented. Sojourner thought it evident he had been taking a drop too much, but as he was civil and good-natured and she did not feel inclined to spend the night in the open air, she felt driven to the necessity of accepting their hospitality, whatever it might prove to be. The woman soon informed her that there was a ball in the place, at which they would like to drop in a while, before they went to their home.

Balls being no part of Sojourner's mission, she was not desirous of attending; but her hostess could be satisfied with nothing short of a taste of it, and she was forced to go with her, or relinquish their company at once, in which move there might be more exposure than in accompanying her. She went, and soon found herself surrounded by an assemblage of people, collected from the very dregs of society, too ignorant and degraded to understand, much less entertain, a high or bright idea, in a dirty hovel, destitute of every comfort, and where the fumes of whisky were abundant and powerful.

Sojourner's guide there was too much charmed with the combined entertainments of the place to be able to tear herself away until she found her faculties for enjoyment failing her, from a too free use of liquor; and she betook herself to bed till she could recover them. Sojourner, seated in a corner, had time for many reflections and refrained from lecturing them in obedience to the recommendation, 'Cast not your pearls', etc.

When the night was far spent, the husband of the sleeping woman aroused the sleeper, and reminded her that she was not very polite to the woman she had invited to sleep at her house, and of the propriety of returning home. They once more emerged into the pure air, which to our friend Sojourner, after so long breathing the noisome air of ballroom, was most refreshing and grateful. Just as day dawned, they reached the place they called their home. Sojourner now saw that she had lost nothing in the shape of rest by remaining so long at the ball, as their miserable cabin afforded but one bunk or pallet for sleeping; and had there been many such, she would have preferred sitting up all night to occupying one like it. They very politely offered her the bed, if she would use, but civilly declining, she waited for morning with an eagerness of desire she never felt before on the subject, and was never more happy than when the eye of day shed its golden light once more over the earth She was once more free, and while daylight should last, independent, and needed no invitation to pursue her journey. Let these facts teach us, that every pedestrian in the world is not a vagabond, and that it is a dangerous thing to compel anyone to receive that hospitality from the vicious and abandoned which they should have received from us, as thousands can testify, who have thus been caught in the snares of the wicked.

The fourth of July, Isabella arrived at Huntingdon; from thence she went to Cold Springs, where she found the people making preparations for a mass temperance meeting. With her usual alacrity, she entered into their labors, getting up dishes a la New York, greatly to the

satisfaction of those she assisted. After remaining at
Cold Springs some three weeks, she returned to
Huntingdon, where she took boat for Connecticut.
Landing at Bridgeport, she again resumed her travels
towards the north-east, lecturing some, and working
some, to get wherewith to pay tribute to Caesar, as she
called it; and in this manner she presently came to the
city of New Haven, where she found many meetings,
which she attended at some of which she was allowed
to express her views freely, and without reservation. She
also called meetings expressly to give herself an
opportunity to be heard; and found in the city many
true friends of Jesus, as she judged, with whom she held
communion of spirit, having no preference for one sect
more than another, but being well satisfied with all who
gave her evidence of having known or loved the
Saviour.

After thus delivering her testimony in this pleasant
city, feeling she had not as yet found an abiding place,
she went from thence to Bristol, at the request of a
zealous sister who desired her to go to the latter place,
and hold a religious conversation with some friends of
hers there. She went as requested, found the people
kindly and religiously disposed, and through them she
became acquainted with several very interesting
persons.

A spiritually-minded brother in Bristol, becoming interested in her new views and original opinions, requested as a favor that she would go to Hartford, to see and converse with friends of his there. Standing ready to perform any service in the Lord, she went to Hartford as desired, carrying in her hand the following note from this brother:

Sister, I send you this loving messenger as I believe her to be one that God loves;. Ethiopia is stretching forth her hands unto God. You can see by this sister that God does by his Spirit alone teach his own children things to come. Please receive her, and she will tell you some new things. Let her tell her story without interrupting her, and give close attention, and you will see she has got the lever of truth, that God helps her to pry where but few can. She cannot read or write, but the law is in her heart.

Send her to our brothers and wherever else she can do the most good.

From your brother, H. L. B.

As soon as Isabella saw God as an all-powerful and pervading spirit, she became desirous of hearing all that had been written of him, and listened to the account of the creation of the world and its first inhabitants, as contained in the first chapters of Genesis, with peculiar interest. For some time she received it all literally, though it appeared strange to her that 'God worked by the day, got tired, and stopped to rest'.. But after a little time she began to reason upon it thus,: "Why, if God works by the day, and one day's work tires him, and he is obliged to rest, either from weariness or on account of darkness, or if he waited for the cool of the day to walk in the garden, because he was inconvenienced by the heat of the sun, why then it seems that God cannot do as much as I can; for I can bear the sun at noon, and work several days and nights in succession without being much tired.

"Or, if he rested nights because of the darkness, it is very queer that he should make the night so dark that he could not see himself If I had been God, I would have made the night light enough for my own convenience, surely."

But the moment she placed this idea of God by the side of the impression she had once so suddenly received of his inconceivable greatness and entire spirituality, that moment she exclaimed mentally, "No, God does not stop to rest for he is a spirit, and cannot tire; he cannot want for light, for he hath all light in himself. And if God is 'all in all' and 'worketh all in all', as I have heard them read, then it is impossible he should rest at all; for if he did, every other thing would stop and rest too; the waters would not flow, and the fishes could not swim; and all motion must cease. God could have no pauses in his work, and he needed no Sabbaths of rest. Man might need them, and he should take them when he needed them, whenever he required rest. As it regarded the worship of God, he was to be worshipped at all times and in all places; and one portion of time never seemed to be more holy than another."

These views, which were the result of the workings of her own mind, assisted solely by the light of her own experience and very limited knowledge, were, for a long time after their adoption, closely locked in her own breast, fearing lest their avowal might bring upon her the imputation of 'infidelity', the usual charge preferred by all religionists, against those who entertain religious views and feelings differing materially from their own. If, from their own sad experience, they are withheld from shouting the cry of 'Infidel'! they fail not to see and to feel, ay, and to say, that the dissenters are not of the right spirit, and that their spiritual eyes have never been unsealed.

While travelling in Connecticut, she met a minister with whom she held a long discussion on these points, as well as on various other topics, such as the origin of

all things, especially the origin of evil, at the same time
bearing her testimony strongly against a paid ministry
— he belonged to that class and, as a matter of course,
as strongly advocated his own side of the question.

I had forgotten to mention, in its proper place, a very
important fact, that when she was examining the
Scriptures, she wished to hear them without comment;
but she employed adult persons to read them to her, and
she asked them to read a passage over again, they
invariably commenced to explain, by giving her their
version of it and in this way, they tried her feelings
exceedingly. As a consequence of this, she ceased to ask
adult persons to read the Bible to her, and substituted
children in their stead. Children, as soon as they could
read distinctly, would re-read the same sentence to her,
as often as she wished, and without comment; and in
that way she was enabled to see what her own mind
could make out of the record, and that, she said, was
what she wanted, and not what others thought it to
mean. She wished to compare the teachings of the Bible
with the witness within her; and she came to the
conclusion, that the spirit of truth spoke in those
records, but that the recorders of those truths had
intermingled with them ideas and suppositions of their
own. This is one among the many proofs of her energy
and independence of character.

When it became known to her children that Sojourner had left New York, they were filled with wonder and alarm. Where could she have gone, and why had she left, were questions no one could answer satisfactorily. Now, their imaginations painted her as a wandering maniac and again they feared she had been left to commit suicide; and many were the tears they shed at the loss of her.

But when she reached Berlin, Conn., she wrote to them informing them of her whereabouts, and waiting an answer to her letter; thus quieting their fears, and gladdening their hearts once more with assurances of her continued life and her love.

In Hartford and vicinity, she met with several persons who believed in the 'second advent' doctrines; or, the immediate personal appearance of Jesus Christ. At first she thought she had never heard of 'second advent'. But when it was explained to her, she recollected having attended Mr. Miller's meeting in New York, where she saw a great many enigmatical pictures hanging on the wall, which she could not understand, and which, being out of the reach of her understanding, failed to interest her. In this section of country, she attended two camp-meetings of the believers in these doctrines. The 'second advent' excitement being then at its greatest height. The last meeting was at Windsor Lock. The people, as a matter of course, eagerly inquired of her concerning her belief, as it regarded the most important tenet. She told them it had not been revealed to her; perhaps, if she could read, she might see it differently. Sometimes, to the eager inquiry of "Oh, don't you believe the Lord is coming?" she answered, "I believe the Lord is as near as he can be, and not be it." With these evasive and non-exciting answers, she kept their minds calm as it respected her unbelief, until she could have an opportunity to hear the views fairly stated, in order to judge more understandingly of this matter, and see if, in her estimation, there was any good ground for expecting an event which was, in the minds of so many, as it were, shaking the very foundations of the universe. She was invited to join them in their religious exercises, and accepted the invitation praying, and talking in her own peculiar style, and attracting many about her by her singing.

When she had convinced the people that she was a lover of God and his cause, and had gained a good standing with them, so that she could get a hearing from them, she had become quite sure in her own mind that they were laboring under a delusion, and she commenced to use her influence to calm the fears of the people and pour oil upon the troubled waters. In one part of the grounds, she found a knot of people greatly excited: she mounted a stump and called out, "Hear! Hear!"

When the people had gathered around her, as they were in a state to listen to anything new, she addressed them as 'children' and asked them why they made such a to-do. "Are you not commanded to watch and pray? You are neither watching nor praying." And she bade them, with the tones of a kind mother, return to the tents, and there watch and pray, without noise or tumult, for the Lord would not come to such a scene of confusion. "The Lord came still and quiet." She assured them, that the Lord might come, move all through the camp, and go away again, and they would never know it, in the state they then were.

They seemed glad to seize upon any reason for being less agitated and distressed, and many of them suppressed their noisy terror, and returned to their tents to watch and pray, begging others to do the same, and listen to the advice of the good sister. She felt she had done some good, and then went to listen further to the preachers. They appeared to her to be doing the utmost to agitate and excite the people, who were already too much excited; and when she had listened till her feelings would let her listen silently no longer, she arose and addressed the preachers. The following are specimens of her speech:

"Here you are talking about being changed in the twinkling of an eye. If the Lord should come, he'd change you to *nothing*, for there is nothing to you.

"You seem to be expecting to go to some parlor away up somewhere, and when the wicked have been burnt, you are coming back to walk in triumph over their ashes — this is to be your New Jerusalem! Now I can't see anything so very nice in that, coming back to such a mess as that would be, a world covered with the ashes of the wicked! Besides, if the Lord comes and burns as you say he will, I am not going away; I am going to stay here and stand the fire, like Shadrach, Meshach, and Abednego! And Jesus will walk with me through the fire, and keep me from harm. Nothing belonging to God can burn any more than God himself; such shall have no need to go away to escape the fire. No, I shall remain. Do you tell me that God's children can't stand fire?" Her manner and tone spoke louder than words, saying, "It is absurd to think so."

The ministers were taken quite aback at so unexpected an opposer, and one of them, in the kindest possible manner, commenced a discussion with her, by

asking her questions, and quoting scripture to her;
concluding finally, that although she had learned
nothing of the great doctrine which was so exclusively
occupying their minds at the time, she had learned
much that man had never taught her.

At this meeting, she received the address of different
persons, residing in various places, with an invitation to
visit them. She promised to go soon to Cabotville, and
started shaping her course for that place. She arrived at
Springfield one evening at six o'clock, and immediately
began to search for a lodging for the night. She walked
from six till past nine, and was then on the road from
Springfield to Cabotville, before she found one
sufficiently hospitable to give her a night under their
roof. Then a man gave her twenty-five cents, and bade
her go to a tavern and stay all night. She did so,
returning in the morning to thank him, assuring him
that she had put his money to its legitimate use. She
found a number of the friends she had seen at Windsor
when she reached the manufacturing town of
Cabotville, (which has lately taken the name of
Chicopee) and with them she spent a pleasant week or
more, after which, she left them to visit the Shaker
village in Enfield. She now began to think of finding a
resting place, at least, for a season; for she had
performed quite a long journey, considering she had

walked most of the way; and she had a mind to look in upon the Shakers and see how things were there, and whether there was any opening there for her. But on her way back to Springfield, she called at a house and asked for a piece of bread; her request was granted, and she was kindly invited to tarry all night, as it was getting late, and she would not be able to stay at every house in that vicinity, which invitation she cheerfully accepted. When the man of the house came in, he recollected having seen her at the camp meeting and repeated some conversations, by which she recognized him again. He soon proposed having a meeting that evening, went out and notified his friends and neighbours who came together, and she once more held forth to them in her peculiar style. Through the agency of this meeting, she became acquainted with several people residing in Springfields to whose houses she was cordially invited, and with whom she spent some pleasant time.

One of these friends, writing of her arrival there, speaks as follows:

"After saying that she and her people belonged to that class of persons who believed in the second advent doctrines, and that this class, believing also in freedom of speech and action, often found at their meetings many singular people, who did not agree with them in their principal doctrine; and that, being thus prepared to hear new and strange things, they listened eagerly to Sojourner and drank in all she said; and she soon became a favorite among them; that when she arose to speak in their assemblies, her commanding figure and dignified manner hushed every trifler into silence and her singular and sometimes uncouth modes of expression never provoked a laugh, but often were the whole audience melted into tears by her touching stories. Many were the lessons of wisdom and faith I have delighted to learn from her. She continued to be a great favorite in our meetings, both on account of her remarkable gift in prayer, and still more remarkable talent for singing, and the aptness and point of her remarks.

"As we were walking the other day, she said she had often thought what a beautiful world this would be, when she should see everything right side up, 'Now, we see everything topsy-turvy, and all is confusion.' For a person who knows nothing of this fact in the science of optics, this seemed quite a remarkable idea.

"We also loved her for her sincere and ardent example, her unwavering faith in God, and her contempt of what; the world calls fashion, and what we call folly.

"She was in search of a quiet place, where a wayward traveller might rest. She had heard of Fruitlands, and was inclined to go there, but the friends she found here thought it best for her to visit Northampton. She passed her time, while with us, working wherever her work was needed, and talking where work was not needed. She would not receive money for her work, saying she worked for the Lord; and if her wants were supplied, she received it as from the Lord.

"She remained with us until far into winter, when we introduced her to the Northampton Association. She wrote to me from thence, that she had found the resting place she had so long desired. And she has remained there ever since."

When Sojourner had been at Northampton a few months, she attended another camp-meeting, at which she performed a very important part.

A party of wild young men, with no motive but that of entertaining themselves by annoying and injuring the feelings of others, had assembled at the meeting, hooting and yelling, and in various ways interrupting the services, and causing much disturbance. Those who had the charge of the meeting, having tried their persuasive powers in vain, grew impatient and tried threatening.

The young men, considering themselves insulted,

collected their friends, to the number of a hundred or more, dispersed themselves through the grounds, making the most frightful noises, and threatening to fire the tents. It was said the authorities of the meeting sat in grave consultation, decided to have the ringleaders arrested, and sent for the constable, to the great displeasure of some of the company, who were opposed to such an appeal to force and arms. Be that as it may, Sojourner, seeing consternation depicted in every countenance, caught the contagion and, ere she was aware, found herself quaking with fear.

Under the impulse of this sudden emotion, she fled to the most retired corner of a tent, and secreted herself behind a trunk, saying to herself, "I am the only colored person here, and on me, probably, their wicked mischief will fall first, and perhaps fatally." But feeling how great was her insecurity even there, as the very tent began to shake from its foundations, she began to soliloquize as follows:

"Shall I run away and hide from the Devil? Me, a servant of the living God? Have I not faith enough to go out and quell that mob, when I know it is written 'One shall chase a thousand, and two put ten thousand to flight'? I know there are not a thousand here, and I know I am a servant of the living God. I'll go to the rescue, and the Lord shall go with and protect me."

She felt as if she had three hearts, and that they were so large, her body could hardly contain them.

She now came forth from her hiding-place, and invited several to go with her and see what they could do to still the raging of the moral elements. They declined, and considered her wild to think of it.

The meeting was in the open fields the full moon shed its saddened light over all, and the woman who was that evening to address them was trembling on the preacher's stand. The noise and confusion were now terrific Sojourner left the tent alone and, unaided, and walking to the top of a small rise of ground, commenced to sing, in her most fervid manner, with all the strength of her most powerful voice, the hymn resurrection of Christ:

It was early in the morning, it was early in
the morning
Just at the break of day
When he rose, when he rose, when he rose,
And went to heaven on a cloud.

All who have ever heard her sing this hymn will probably remember it as long as they remember her. The hymn, the tune, the style, are each too closely associated with her to be easily separated from her, and when sung in one of her most animated moods, in the open air, with the utmost strength of her most powerful voice, must have been truly thrilling.

As she commenced to sing, the young men made a rush towards her, and she was immediately encircled by a dense body of the rioters, many of them armed with sticks or clubs as their weapons of defence, if not of attack. As the circle narrowed around her, she ceased singing, and after a short pause, inquired, in a gentle but fine tone, "Why do you come about me with clubs and sticks? I am not doing harm to anyone."

"We aren't going to hurt you, old woman; we came to hear you sing," cried many voices simultaneously.

"Sing to us, old woman," cried one.

"Talk to us, old woman," said another.

"Pray for us, old woman," said a third.

"Tell us your experiences."

"You stand and smoke so near me, I cannot sing or talk," she answered.

"Stand back," said several authoritative voices, with not most gentle or courteous accompaniments, raising their rude weapons in the air.

The crowd suddenly moved back, and the circle became larger, as many voices again called for singing, talking, or praying, backed by assurances that no one would be allowed to hurt her — the speakers declaring with an oath that they would knock down any person who would offer her the least indignity.

She looked about her, and with her usual discrimination said inwardly: 'Here must be many young men in all this assemblage, bearing within them hearts susceptible of good impressions. I will speak to them.'

She did speak. They silently heard, and civilly asked her many questions. It seemed to her to be given to her at the time to answer them with truth and wisdom beyond herself. Her speech had operated on the roused passions of the mob like oil on agitated waters; they were, as a whole, entirely subdued, and only clamored when she ceased to speak or sing. Those who stood in the background, after the circle was enlarged, cried out, "Sing aloud, old woman, we can't hear." Those who held the sceptre of power among them requested that she should make a pulpit of a neighboring wagon. She said, "If I do, they'll overthrow it."

"No, they sha'n't, he who dares hurt you, we'll knock him down instantly, damn him," cried the chief.

"No we won't, no we won't, nobody shall hurt you," answered the many voices of the mob. They kindly assisted her to mount the wagon, from which she spoke and sung to them for about an hour. Of all she said to them on the occasion, she remembers only the following:

"Well, there are two congregations on this ground. It is written that there shall be a separation, and the sheep shall be separated from the goats. The other preachers have the sheep, I have the goats. And I have a few sheep among my goats, but they are very ragged."

This produced great laughter. When she became wearied with talking, she began to contrive some way to induce them to disperse. While she paused, they loudly clamored for her to sing some more.

She motioned them to be quiet, and called out to them.

"Children, I have talked and sung to you as you asked me, and now I have a request to make if you will grant it."

"Yes, yes, yes," resounded in every quarter.

"Well, it is this," she continued, "I will sing one more hymn for you, will you then go and leave us this night in peace?"

"Yes, yes," came faintly, feebly from a few.

"I repeat it," said Sojourner, "and I want an answer from you all, as of one accord. If I will sing you one more, you will go away, and leave us this night in peace?"

"Yes, yes, yes," shouted many voices with hearty emphasis. "I repeat my request once more," said she, "and I want you all to answer."

And she reiterated the words again. This time a long, loud "Yes!" came up, as from the multitudinous mouth of the entire mob.

"Amen! It is sealed," repeated Sojourner, in the deepest and most solemn tones of her powerful and sonorous voice. Its effect ran through the multitude, like an electric shock; and most of them considered themselves bound by their promise, as they might have failed to do under less imposing circumstances. Some of them began instantly to leave, others said, "Are we not to have one more hymn?"

"Yes," answered their entertainer, and she commenced to sing:

> I bless the Lord I've got my seal today and
> today
> To slay Goliath in the field today and today
> The good old way is a righteous way
> I mean to take the kingdom in the good old
> way.

While singing, she heard some enforcing obedience to their promises while a few seemed refusing to abide by it. But before she had quite concluded, she saw them turn from her, and in the course of a few minutes, they were running as fast as they well could in a solid body; and she says she can only compare them to nothing but a swarm of bees, so dense was their phalanx, so straight their course, so hurried their march. As they passed with a rush very near the stand of the other preachers, the hearts of the people were smitten with fear, thinking that their entertainer had failed to enchain them longer with her spell, and that they were coming upon them with re-doubled and remorseless fury. But they found they were mistaken, and that their fears were groundless; for, before they could well recover from their surprise, every rioter was gone, and not one was left on the grounds, or seen there again during the meeting.

Sojourner was informed that as her audience reached the main road, some distance from the tents, a few of the rebellious spirits refused to go on, and proposed returning, but their leaders said, "We have promised to leave, we all promised, and we must go, all go, and none of us shall return again."

She did not fall in love at first sight with the Northampton Association, for she arrived there at a time when appearances did not correspond with the ideas of associationists, as they had been spread out in their writings, for their phalanx was a factory, and they were wanting in means to carry out their ideas of beauty and elegance as they would have done in different circumstances. But she thought she would make an effort to tarry with them one night, though that seemed to her no desirable affair. But as soon as she saw that accomplished, literary and refined persons were living in that plain and simple manner, and submitting to the labors and privations incident to such an infant institution, she said, "Well, if these can live here, I can."

Afterwards, she gradually became pleased with, and attached to, the place and the peoples as well she might; for it must have been no small thing to have found a home in a community composed of some of the choicest spirits of the age, where all was characterized by an equality of feeling, a liberty of thought and speech, and a largeness of soul, she could not have before met with, to the same extent, in any of her wanderings.

Our first knowledge of her was derived from a friend who had resided for a time in the community and who, after describing her, and singing one of her hymns, wished that we might see her. But we little thought, at that time, that we should ever pen these simple annals of this child of nature.

When we first saw her, she was working with a hearty goodwill; saying she would not be induced to take regular wages, believing, as once before, that now Providence had provided her with a never-failing fount, from which her every want might be perpetually supplied through her mortal life.

In this, she had calculated too fast. For the Associationists found that, taking everything into consideration, they would find it most expedient to act individually; and again, the subject of this sketch found her dreams unreal, and herself flung back upon her own resources for the supply of her needs. This she might have found more inconvenient at her time of life for labor, exposure and hardship had made sad inroads upon her iron constitution, by inducing chronic disease and premature old age had she not remained under the shadow of one who never wearies in doing good, giving to the needy, and supplying the wants of the destitute. She has now set her heart upon having a little home of her own, even at this late hour of life, where she may feel a greater freedom than she can in the house of another, and where she can repose a little, after her day of action has passed by. And for such a home she is now dependent on the charities of the benevolent, and to them we appeal with confidence.

Through all the scenes of her eventful life may be traced the energy of a naturally powerful mind — the fearlessness and childlike simplicity of one untrammelled by education or conventional customs — purity of character, an unflinching adherence to principle, and a native enthusiasm which, under different circumstances, might easily have produced another Joan of Arc.

With all her fervor, enthusiasm and speculation, her religion is not tinctured in the least with gloom. No doubt, no hesitation, no despondency, spreads a cloud over her soul; but all is bright, clear, positive, and at times ecstatic. Her trust is in God, and from him she looks for good, and not evil. She feels that perfect love casteth out fear.

Having more than once found herself awaking from a mortifying delusion, as in the case of the Sing-Sing kingdom, and resolving not to be thus deluded again, she has set suspicion to guard the door of her heart, and allows it perhaps to be aroused by too slight causes, on certain subjects her vivid imagination assisting to magnify the phantoms of her fears into gigantic proportions much beyond their real size; instead of resolutely adhering to the rule we all like best, when it is to be applied to ourselves; that of placing everything we see to the account of the best possible motive, until time and circumstance prove that we were wrong. Where no good motive can be assigned, it may become our duty to suspend our judgment until evidence can be had.

In the application of this rule, it is an undoubted

duty to exercise a commendable prudence, by refusing to repose any important trust to the keeping of persons who may be strangers to us, and whose trustworthiness we have never seen tried. No possible good, but incalculable evil may and does arise from the too common practice of placing all conduct, the source of which we do not fully understand, to the worst of intentions. How often is the gentle, timid soul discouraged, and driven perhaps to despondency, by finding its 'good evil spoken of' and a well-meant but mistaken action loaded with an evil design.

If the world would but assiduously set about reforming itself on this one point, who can calculate the change it would produce, the evil it would annihilate, and the happiness it would confer. None but an all-seeing eye could at once embrace so vast a result. A result, how desirable, and one that can be brought about only by the most simple process — that of every individual seeing to it that he commit not this sin himself. For why should we all allow in ourselves the very fault we most dislike, when committed against us? Shall we not at least aim at consistency?

Had she possessed less generous self-sacrifice, more knowledge of the world and of business matters in general, and had she failed to take it for granted that others were like herself, and would, when her turn came to need, do as she had done, and find it more blessed to give than to receive, she might have laid by something for the future. For few, perhaps, have ever possessed the power and inclinations in the same degree, at one and the same time, to labor as she has done, both day and night, for so long a period of time. And had these energies been well-directed, and the proceeds well-husbanded, since she has been her own mistress they would have given herself an independence during her natural life. But her constitutional biases, and her early training, or rather want of training, prevented this result; and it is too late now to remedy the great mistake. Shall she then be left to want? Who will not answer, "No."

'O glory, glory, glory, won't you come along with me?'

'Sojourner,' said the Professor to her one day, when he heard her singing, 'you seem to be very sure about Heaven.'

'Well, I be,' she answered, triumphantly.

'What makes you so sure there is any Heaven?'

'Well, 'cause I got such a hankering after it in here,' she said, giving a thump on her breast with her usual energy.

In the spring of 1849, Sojourner made a visit to her eldest daughter, Diana, who has ever suffered from ill health, and remained with Mr. Dumont, Isabella's humane master She found him still living, though advanced in age, and reduced in property (as he had been for a number of years), but greatly enlightened on the subject of slavery. He said he could then see, that slavery was the wickedest thing in the world, the greatest curse the earth had ever felt, that it was then very clear to his mind that it was so, though, while he was a slaveholder himself, he did not see it so, and thought it was as right as holding any other property.

Sojourner remarked to him, that it might be the same with those who are now slaveholders.

"O, no," replied he, with warmth, "it cannot be. For now, the sin of slavery is so clearly written out, and so much talked against,(why, the whole world cries out against it!) that if any one says he don't know, and has not heard, he must, I think, be a liar. In my slaveholding days, there were few that spoke against it, and these few made little impression on anyone. Had it been as it is now, think you I could have held slaves? No! I should not have dared to do it, but should have emancipated every one of them. Now, it is very different; all may hear if they will."

She received a letter from her daughter Diana, dated Hyde Park, December 19, 1849, which informed her that Mr Dumont had gone West with some of his sons — that he had taken along with him, probably through mistake, the few articles of furniture she had left with him.

"Never mind," said Sojourner, "what we give to the poor, we lend to the Lord."

She thanked the Lord with fervor, that she had lived to hear her master say such blessed things. She recalled the lectures he used to give his slaves, on speaking the truth and being honest, and laughing, she said, "He taught us not to lie and steal, when he was stealing all the time himself and did not know it. Oh, how sweet to my mind was this confession. And what a confession for a master to make to a slave. A slaveholding master turned to a brother. Poor old man, may the Lord bless him, and all slaveholders partake of his spirit.

WHAT THE PAPER SAY ABOUT SOJOURNER TRUTH:

Sojourner has been some months in New York, speaking in many places with great acceptance, and is now in this city, where she will speak this evening in the lecture room of the Unitarian Church, corner of Lafayette Avenue and Shelby Street. Let those who enjoy an original entertainment hear her. She is trying to pay off a mortgage on her little house in Battle Creek. Give her a full house, and a generous contribution. Remember that here in the North, in the State of New York, she was robbed, by our race and by our laws, of forty years of her life. Do we not owe her, from abundant fullness, some compensation for those years with their entailed sorrow?

A New York paper.

Sojourner Truth, whom the newspapers lately described as dying, reported herself in person to us alive and well, a living contradiction of the false rumor.

The old lady says that, so far from being at the point of death, she has not experienced for many months any symptom of sickness. Her age is now eighty, but her spirit continues as youthful as ever. On Sunday morning she heard Mr. Beecher's opening sermon of the season, which she called a feast for her poor old soul.

From a Brooklyn paper.

Sojourner's conversation is witty, sarcastic, sensible, and oftentimes profound. Her varied experience during a long life gives her a rich and deep fountain to draw upon for the entertainment and instruction of her friends, and her reminiscences and comments are equally interesting both to grown folks and children. She looks and acts as if she might live to be a hundred years old. She has uplifted her voice to two generations of mankind, and may yet become prophetess to a third.

Don't come expecting fine rhetoric, finished grammar, or dictionary pronunciation; but if you want to hear an earnest soul of eighty or more years, on the borders of the coming world, still young in the graces of Christian charity, and ardent in the work assigned her, talk of right and justice, and set them forth with a spirit and skill that learned men might well envy, turn out tonight.

From a New Jersey paper

Springfield, Union County, New Jersey, and its Presbyterian Church were honored on Wednesday night by the presence of that lively old negro mummy whose age ranges from eighty to over a hundred, Sojourner Truth. Fifty years ago she was considered a crazy woman who was wont to address street meetings. She was smuggled into the church by some pious radical to give her religious experience; and she did it, rather to the confusion and disgust of the audience. When respectable churches consent to admit to the houses opened for the worship of God, every wandering negro minstrel or street spouter who may profess to have a peculiar religious experience, or some grievance to redress, render themselves justly liable to public ridicule.

From a New Jersey paper

She is a crazy, ignorant, repelling negress, and her guardians would do a Christian act to restrict her entirely to private life.

From our Springfield correspondent

Sojourner Truth is the name of a man now lecturing in Kansas City. He could only be called a 'sojourner' there, for truth could not abide in that place long as a permanent resident.

The St. Louis Despatch